Table of Contents

Table of Contents, Continued

Reverend John Harper

The Titanic's Last Hero

Moody Adams

with historian Lee W. Merideth

The Titanic's Last Hero
By Moody Adams

Copyright © 2012, Rocklin Press

First Rocklin Press edition
10 9 8 7 6 5 4 3 2 1

ISBN 978-0-9836103-1-1

Cover photo and design: Jim Zach

Cover:
Titanic model built by Stephen W. Henniger, 1996-97
Diorama setting by William E. Hitchcock, 1996-97
Collection of the Ships of the Sea Museum, Savannah, GA

The "The Titanic's Last Hero" may be purchased in discounted quantities for Christian, educational or promotional use. Contact:

Rocklin Press
An imprint of
Historical Indexes Publishing Co.
7501 Palm Avenue #169
Yucca Valley, CA 92284
rocklinpress@earthlink.net
phone: 408-393-1606

Dedicated to:

Bill Guthrie
of Glasgow, Scotland,

a concerned Christian who kept the story of John Harper alive. He collected materials, questioned acquaintances and even attended the funeral of John Harper's daughter. Without his research and work, this book would not have been possible. He has rendered a great service to the work of Jesus Christ.

Testimonies and tributes in this book were originally published in Scotland in 1912. John Climie compiled and edited them at the request of John Harper's brother, George.

Scriptures are quoted from The King James Bible.

John Harper: A Hero on the Titanic. Originally published ©1997 by the Moody Adams Evangelistic Association. For information, address the Moody Adams Evangelistic Association, 11715 Bricksome Ave. B-3, Baton Rouge, LA 70816 or send fax to 504-939-3135.

Preface

John Harper had been dead for 85 years when he changed my life dramatically. In 1997, I was in the Harper Memorial Baptist Church in Glasgow, which was renamed for their heroic first pastor, John Harper. There I met Bill Guthrie, a member of the church, who has a fantastic knowledge of Harper. Guthrie furnished me with a rare copy of the original book on Harper, church documents and related accounts from people whose families had known this heroic Scotsman.

My personal experience with Harper's story made me determined to pass it on to as many people as possible. This is done with the conviction that the life of John Harper is capable of leaving an indelible imprint upon all who become acquainted with his passionate passage through this world.

Harper stood as a giant of unselfishness in a world where most men are obsessed with looking out for "number one," a giant of sacrifice in a world where most men are unwilling to deprive themselves, a giant of passion for souls in a world where few men possess a deep desire for the salvation of their fellow men.

The testimonies and tributes in this book were printed under the title *John Harper: A Man of God*. John Climie wrote the 1912 preface, the second chapter and compiled the comments of acquaintances and converts who knew John Harper. Their writing was done at the request of Pastor

George Harper, the brother of John Harper. These original accounts have been edited very little to preserve the 1912 Scottish style.

Joseph Addison, an English essayist, said, "Unbounded courage and compassion . . . make the hero and the man complete." Harper embodied the courage and compassion that made the complete hero.

Moody Adams

A Preface To

John Harper: A Man of God
Published in 1912

The editorship of this volume has been undertaken at the request of Pastor George Harper, who has rendered most valuable assistance, and whose tender and loving tribute to the memory of his brother will be read with special interest. As the biography is composed mainly of tributes by various writers it has been impossible to avoid duplication. But it has been considered proper that the tributes should appear as written, since each contributor writes from his own standpoint.

The sinking of the *Titanic* with its living freight has created a wail of sorrow throughout the civilized world. The idea of 1522 lives being lost through the sinking of one ship is perfectly appalling. Even after the great ship was at the bottom of the sea, the newspapers, not knowing what had taken place, were announcing that the *Titanic* was "absolutely unsinkable." But the forces of nature were too much for the mammoth liner. The waters in the Polar regions had, under the keen breath of the north wind, massed themselves together, and from that ice zone came floating silently along the huge berg that ripped the steamer's bottom and sent it to its ocean bed. "By the breath of God frost is given: and the breadth of the waters is straitened" *(Job 37:10)*. The iceberg straitened the Atlantic tract, and the great ship was sent to the bottom of the sea. That Mr. Harper should have been taken away in his prime has perplexed many.

We had ventured frequently within the past few years to predict for him a great future of usefulness, but:

> "We know not what awaits us.
> God kindly veils our eyes."

We reverently bow our heads under the shadow of this great calamity that has bereaved us of one who lived not for himself, but for the glory of Him who redeemed him with His own precious blood.

It is hoped that this small memento of a life lived for God and for the good of his fellow-men will carry a blessing with it, and be a stimulus to many. In this hope it is sent forth.

John Climie

John Harper

*While the flames of other ambitions
flickered and died,
John Harper's burned even brighter
as he sank into a watery grave.
When death forced others to face
the folly of their life's pursuits,
John Harper's goal of winning men to
Jesus Christ became more vital as he
breathed his final breaths.*

Chapter 1

Going Out In a Blaze of Glory

As the dark, freezing waters of the Atlantic crept slowly up the decks of the *Titanic*, John Harper shouted, "Let the women, children and the unsaved into the lifeboats." Harper took his life jacket—the final hope of survival—and gave it to another man. After the ship had disappeared beneath the dark water, leaving Harper floundering in the icy waters, he was heard urging those about him to put their faith in Jesus Christ.

It was the night of April 14, 1912, a night for heroes, and John Harper met the challenge. Though the waters swallowing him were bitterly cold and the sea about him was dark, John Harper left this world in a brilliant blaze of glory.

Harper's heroics were spontaneous. He had no reason to expect the *Titanic* to sink, nor time to write a script. A trade magazine, *The Shipbuilder*, labeled the *Titanic* "practically unsinkable." On May 31, 1911, an employee of the White Star Line Company said, "Not even God Himself could sink this ship." The *Titanic* reflected all the security, luxury and confidence of the Victorian-Edwardian era. The Associated Press was sold on the ship, declaring, "All that wealth and modern workmanship could produce was embodied in the *Titanic*, the longest vessel ever built, over 4 city blocks in length . . . with accommodations for a crew of 860 and a passenger capacity of 3,500, she was built with as much care as is put into the finest chronometers." The *Titanic's* lavish extravagance and record-breaking size awed the golden age of shipbuilding. Her 50,000 hp engines that produced the 24 knots-per-hour speed were secured in sixteen water tight compartments. Each was protected by steel bulkheads. At the time of her launch, *Titanic* was the world's largest man-made movable object. After making its first two passenger and mail stops at Cherbourg, France and Queenstown, Ireland, passengers gained an increased sense of security. Harper wrote a letter to his friend Charles Livingtone before docking at Queenstown, saying, "Thus far the passage is all that can be desired."

At 11:40 p.m. April 14, 1912, an iceberg scraped the ship's starboard side, showering the decks with ice and ripping open six water-tight compartments. The sea poured in. Most passengers remained unconvinced that the *Titanic* would go down until the crew started shooting flares into the air. As Lee Merideth said, "In the pitch-black and cloudless sky all you could see were stars, millions of stars and little else. The entire stage consisted of one huge ship blazing with lights slowly sinking into the water bow first and the occasional blindingly white rocket bursting high over the top of the ship as if reaching out to those stars. Almost everyone knew that those who were in the lifeboats were probably going to survive but the mass of people huddled on the deck were going to die. Some of those people were not going to go quietly." After the flares, no one had to be persuaded to enter the lifeboat. Suddenly, when the water had crept halfway to the bridge, a crashing noise, resembling a million pieces of china breaking, jarred the night. As the stern of the *Titanic* rose high in the sky to prepare for her plunge to the ocean floor, a tremendous noise like an explosion jarred the night air. Passengers joined hands and leaped into the water. At 2:20 a.m. *Titanic* began her slow descent to the ocean floor, leaving a mushroom-like cloud of smoke and steam above her grave. In the icy waters of the North Atlantic, in the dead of night, the most famous ship in the world ended her one and only voyage but gained a nautical mystique second only to Noah's ark. It all happened so fast, that Harper could only react. His response left an historic example of courage and faith. "The heroes of mankind," said A. P. Stanley, "are the mountains, the highlands of the moral world." Such a hero was John Harper.

The Hardest Part of his Heroism

It is never easy to undertake such heroic actions, and for John Harper it was exceptionally difficult. His young daughter, Anna Jessie, known as 'Nina' or 'Nana' was traveling with him. Four years earlier, her mother had taken ill and died. Now, Harper knew, Nina was to be left an orphan at six years of age.

When the alarm sounded the end of the *Titanic*, Harper immediately handed Nina to an upper deck captain with instructions to get her in a lifeboat. Then he set out to help others. Nina was rescued and returned to Scotland, where she grew up, married a minister, and dedicated her entire life to the Lord her father had served.

Once, after Harper narrowly missed drowning at 26, he said, "The fear of death did not for one moment disturb me. I believed that sudden death would be sudden glory, but, there was a wee motherless girl in Glasgow." Now, that wee girl was to be motherless *and* fatherless. This had to be the hardest part for Harper.

The Hero in Contrast

This Scotsman's selfless heroism is accentuated by the contrasting conduct of many fellow passengers on this death voyage. While Harper gave up his life jacket, an American banker managed to get a pet dog into a lifeboat, leaving 1,503 humans unaided. There was little of the "go-down-with-the-ship" spirit. Of the 705 saved, 193 were, in fact, men of the crew. Colonel John Jacob Astor asked to join his pregnant wife in a lifeboat and had to be refused by Second Officer Charles Lightoller. Astor was the richest man on the ship, but he was powerless to make his way into a measly little lifeboat. Third Class passenger Daniel Buckley supposedly disguised himself as a woman in an effort to gain a place in a lifeboat. First Class passengers on the first lifeboat to be lowered refused to turn back to pick up people who were drowning, though there was space for many others to have been saved. Mrs. Rosa Abbott, the only woman to go down with the ship and survive, said a man tried to climb up on her back forcing her down under the water and nearly drowning her.

Mr. Bruce Ismay, part owner of the *Titanic* and a managing director of the White Star Line Company and the man responsible for not putting enough lifeboats on board, became the most infamous seaman since Captain Bligh. He crawled into a lifeboat while hundreds of women remained on the dying ship. Captain Smith ordered his men to, "Do your best for the women and children, and look out for yourselves." At the same time John Harper was ordering men to do their best for the women and children and look out for *others*.

An Unwavering Ambition

As the monstrous iceberg ripped the ambitions of others to pieces, Harper demonstrated his unwavering ambition that even death could not affect. He declared Jesus Christ as man's hope to the end. This contrasted others who were forced to face the folly of their ambitions. Mr. Michel Navratil, (traveling under the name Hoffman) had abducted his young children, Michel and Edmond, who became known as the "*Titanic* waifs. His one ambition in life was to get his children away from their wayward mother. But, in the face of death, he put them aboard a lifeboat, assuring that they would be returned to their mother in Nice, France. With his last words he said: "Tell your mother I will always be hers." John Phillips, a self-sufficient crew member, told the *Californian* to "shut up" after they radioed their sixth warning of icebergs in the path of the *Titanic*. Facing death, his ambitious independence disappeared as he cried, "God forgive me . . . God forgive me." The designer of the *Titanic* spent the closing moments of his life in the smoking-room, looking at a mural on the wall with the caption: "Plymouth Harbor." His lifejacket was laid to one side, signifying the end of what had been a beautiful dream on the part of the designer, the ship's owners, and the public.

Mrs. Isador Straus, whose husband owned Macy's Department Store, did not get into a lifeboat. She said to her husband, "Where you go, I go." They helped her maid into boat number eight and put her fur coat on her shoulders, telling her, "Keep warm. I won't be needing it."

Benjamin Guggenheim and his valet Victor Giglio, appeared on deck in full evening dress like two vain comics, saying, "We've dressed in our best and are prepared to go down like gentlemen."

The card sharks, who sailed under assumed names and clipped the passengers for $30,000, stopped their cons. Fitness instructor T. W. McCawley, who was teaching people to ride on mechanical horses and camels, stopped his lesson. The allure of four-postered beds, designer fireplaces, Turkish baths with gilded cooling rooms and the first swimming pool ever built in an ocean liner ended. Passengers in the first-class lounge ceased their partying and paraded onto the deck with lifebelts over their evening dress. The business deals stopped. The chatter of the socialites ceased. But, with his last breath, John Harper tirelessly continued his life's work of urging men to "Believe on the Lord Jesus Christ."

Harper Knew Well the Terrors of Drowning

Harper's courage did not come from ignorance. Probably no one on the *Titanic* was as familiar with the terrors of drowning as John Harper. At two and a half he had fallen into a well and was resuscitated just in time by his mother. At twenty-six Harper was swept out to sea by a reverse current and barely survived. At thirty-two he faced death on a leaking ship in the Mediterranean. Perhaps, it was God's way of testing this servant for his last-warning mission on the *Titanic*.

Harper already knew what hundreds discovered on that tragic night-drowning is a horrible death. One of the *Titanic's* officers was unable to face a slow demise in the water and shot himself to death as the bridge of the ship slipped under. Many of the 1,503 men, women and children left on board screamed their way toward a dreadful silence. In contrast, a confident John Harper faced death with absolute assurance that Jesus had conquered death and given him the gift of eternal life. This assurance overcame the terrors of drowning.

The Passion of his Entire Life

Harper's heroism was not just one shining moment in an otherwise un-heroic existence. He burned, wept, prayed and worked unselfishly for others throughout his entire life. Harper reclaimed drunkards, gamblers, and former prize fighters. As a pastor, he would sometimes spend the entire night in his church praying for his hundreds of members by name. Harper worked day and night, in homes and on the streets, pointing the downtrodden to a better life. He labored ceaselessly among the common people, seeking to care for them.

Harper's tiresome labors were done in spite of bad health. In the summer of 1905, illness stopped him for six months, broke his health and stole his rich resonant voice. His body was never the same, remaining a skeleton of the man he had been. Harper's sallow complexion, fragile frame and repeated illnesses were the marks of one who refused to stop for rest. Yet, despite ill health and a weary body, Harper was bright and joyful. This diligent servant was said to have "gloried in his weakness." The night before *Titanic* sank, while others played and rested, John Harper was seen on the ship deck earnestly seeking to lead a young man to faith in Christ.

Harper Had an Opportunity to Escape the *Titanic*

John Harper's heroics on the *Titanic* take on an added dimension when you consider his opportunity to have avoided the ill-fated ship. Harper was originally scheduled to sail on the Lusitania to preach in Chicago's Moody Memorial Church. Instead, he got up and informed the men at the Seaman's Center Mission in Glasgow the schedule had been changed and he was leaving on the *Titanic* for Chicago. In 1911 he had the best meetings there since the days of the great D. L. Moody, and the church had invited him back for three months of meetings.

Mr. Robert English stood up in a meeting at the Seaman's Center and begged Harper not to make the trip to Chicago. English told Harper he had been in prayer and had an ominous impression that disaster awaited him if he took his voyage. He offered to pay for his ticket if he would delay his trip. Several others have attested to the fact that English pled with Harper; these include Willie Burns, who was actually present at the Glasgow meeting, and English's two granddaughters, Mary Whitelaw and Georgina Smith, both current members of the Harper Memorial Church.

English's words were strikingly similar to those spoke to the Apostle Paul by a prophet named Agabus 1,900 years earlier. Agabus tied his hands and feet, saying: *"So shall the Jews at Jerusalem bind the man that owneth this girdle and shall deliver him into the hands of the Gentiles."* Harper's refusal to turn back was much like Paul's response, *"What mean ye to weep and to break mine heart? for I am ready not to be bound only, but also to die at Jerusalem for the name of the Lord Jesus"* (Acts 21:10-13). Both Paul and Harper had a sense of Divine purpose regarding their trips, and both were willing to die to carry out that purpose.

The prophetic warnings given these two men of God indicate that the Lord sanctioned their sacrifice. Agabus' warning imparted a sense of Divine purpose to Paul as he traveled to Jerusalem where he would preach the gospel, be arrested and sentenced to die. Mr. English's warning gave Harper the same sense of Divine purpose as he became a final witness on a ship of death.

In the End There Were Only
Two Classes of Passengers

Following the sinking of the *Titanic*, the White Star Line office in Liverpool, England placed a large board on either side of the main entrance. On one they printed in large letters, "KNOWN TO BE SAVED," and on the other, "KNOWN TO BE LOST." When the *Titanic's* voyage began there were three classes of passengers. But, when it ended the number was reduced to only two—those who were "saved" by the rescue boats and those who were "lost" in the deep waters.

Relatives and friends of the ship's passengers waited outside the White Star Line office. As news of a passenger came they would print their name on a piece of cardboard. Then an employee carried the name out to the gate. As he faced the crowd and held up the cardboard, a deathly stillness crept over the crowd. They anxiously watched to see on which of the boards the name would be placed.

John Harper plunged into death with reckless abandon, knowing he would be among the lost passengers. But he had absolute confidence that his name would be on the "saved" list at the throne of God. Lord Mersey expressed Harper's attitude toward death exactly, "In a single night, between sunset and sunrise, during a few short hours of oblivion to many unconscious slumbers, there had passed away from this earth hundreds of lives, some rich in promise with apparent happy futures, carrying with them all the hopes of other lives. But the Christian constancy and courage, the absolute self-renunciation and unflinching heroism with which so many met their doom, help us to realize that death is not the end of all things and that this life is but the entrance into the true life, that it is but the portal of eternity."

John Harper's Last Convert

Two hours and forty minutes after the *Titanic* struck the iceberg, she sank beneath the icy waters. Hundreds huddled in lifeboats and rafts, and others clutched pieces of wood hoping to survive until help came. For fifty terrifying minutes the cries for help filled the night. Eva Hart said, "The sound of people drowning is something I cannot describe to you. And neither can anyone else. It is the most dreadful sound. And there is a dreadful silence that follows it." Survivor Colonel Archibald Gracie called this, "The most pathetic and horrible scene of all. The piteous cries of those around us still ring in my ears, and I will remember them to my dying day."

During those final fifty minutes, George Henry Cavell, who was clinging to a board drifted near John Harper. Harper, who was struggling in the water, cried, *"Are you saved?"* The answer returned, *"No."* Harper shouted words from the Bible: *"Believe on the Lord Jesus Christ and thou shalt be saved."* Before responding, the man drifted into the darkness.

Later, the current brought them back in sight of each other. Once more the dying Harper shouted the question, *"Are you saved?"* Once again he received the answer, *"No."* Harper repeated the words of *Acts 16:31, "Believe on the Lord Jesus Christ and thou shalt be saved."* Then the drowning Harper slipped into his watery grave. The man he sought to win put his faith in Jesus Christ. Later he was rescued by the S.S. *Carpathia's* lifeboats. In Hamilton, Ontario, George Henry Cavell testified that he was John Harper's "last convert."

Harper's last convert was won by Harper's last words, *"Believe on the Lord Jesus Christ and thou shalt be saved."*

There were many heroes on the *Titanic*, but, helping others as he drowned, John Harper was the last.

Annie Jessie 'Nina' Harper

*He did one thing then,
and he did it to the end—
he laboured to bring men
from sin to God.*

Chapter 2

The Making Of a Hero
by John Climie

It must be about twenty years, probably slightly more, since we first met Mr. Harper. Our earliest recollection of meeting him was in connection with his labours in the Gospel at Bridge-of-Weir. He then looked simply like a full-grown boy. But at that time, as all through his public career, the candle of the Lord burned brightly in his heart.

John Harper's Conversion

He was born in Houston, Renfrewshire, on 29th May, 1872, and it was on the last Sunday of March, 1886, when he was thirteen years and ten months old that he was led to Jesus. He never knew what it was to sow "wild oats." His young life from his early teens was molded and shielded by his belief in the Lord Jesus Christ. The love of God was shed abroad in his heart, and it pervaded his life to its utmost circumference, shaping his thoughts, in due time spurring him to action, and preserving him from the evil that is in this world. It was through *John 3:16*, "For God so loved the world that He gave His only begotten Son, that who-so-ever believeth in Him, should not perish, but have everlasting life," that the way of salvation was made clear to his heart and mind. It has been the means of enlightening multitudes. It enlightened him, and freed him from fear. "Perfect love casteth out fear."

He received the truth in the love of it, and the truth made him free. In the illuminating words of that text he saw Jesus as God's gift offered to the whole world, and therefore to him as one living in this world. He received that gift with thanksgiving, and for him a new era began.

Those who conducted the public service at which he was led to the Saviour have been blessed to many, but such converts as John Harper are few and far between. There is sometimes great jubilation and multiplied Hallelujahs when some notorious sinner professes conversion, but often-times alas! the re-joicing is short lived. Some, who have been much rejoiced over, have been afterwards found to be far from reliable.

Whether there was any special rejoicing when the village boy that night trusted Jesus cannot be recalled, but in an honest heart, having received the Word, he kept it, and brought forth fruit with patience. The word of *John 15:16* may well have been spoken of him, "I have chosen you, and ordained you, that ye should go and bring forth fruit, and that your fruit should remain."

It is not necessary that men should have plunged deeply into sin to be of special use for Christ after the saving grace of God overtakes them. Mr. Harper in the exercise of his public ministry could never tell of having wandered far from God, and far into sin. Yet under God he was the means of leading numbers to the Saviour who had gone far astray. From his early days he was by God's appointment, very manifestly, "a vessel unto honour, sanctified, and meet for the Master's use."

It is to the Saviour's praise that He can, and that He does, change the lives of men who have dis-graced and dishonoured themselves, and give them a place of honour and distinction in His service. But their deeds of darkness prior to conversion are some-times a snare to them after conversion, rather than a help to them in service for Christ. A clean life before conversion is a valuable asset.

The Heritage of Godly Parents

John Harper was born and brought up in a Christian home, as will be told elsewhere in this book. His parents, poor in this world, were heirs of the Kingdom which God hath promised to them that love Him. The more Christian homes there are the better, not only for the church, but for the nation as well. To be brought up in the nurture and admonition of the Lord, and in an atmosphere of prayer, and of reverence for the Word of God, is to be stamped in youth with impressions that are of great value, even though as is sometimes the case the results looked for are long in appearing.

A godly upbringing is a priceless heritage. While it was on a Sunday night in March, 1886, that the boy in his fourteenth year was led to Christ there were all the impressions of the years that had gone before stored up in his youthful mind. It was not for nothing that he had listened through these impressionable years to his father's prayers and pleadings, and exposition of the Word of God, in that humble home. The fuel had been laid on the hearth of his heart, and lo, on that Sunday night a spark of love divine fell on it, and the flame was kindled.

Harper's Baptism of Fire

During the four years that followed there was nothing particularly noticeable about him, nothing at least that betokened or presaged the great usefulness that marked his future life. He attended regularly the Gospel meetings which were carried on with enthusiasm by some young men in the village, with the help of preachers from different parts. He kept himself free from entangling companionships, and in a quiet and unostentatious way kept the faith.

But after four years and four months, when he had just turned eighteen years of age, an enlarged experience was entered into. Growth is a law of the Kingdom of God. Sometimes it is very slow and scarcely perceptible. At other times it is phenomenally rapid. Some men grow more in an hour in the apprehension of the things of God than others do in years. Such a crisis has sometimes been called "The second blessing, " sometimes "The baptism of fire." By these and other terms preachers and writers have endeavoured to describe the marvelous change that has been suddenly manifested in the lives of some Christian men and women. But by whatever name the new experience may be called it is manifestly the Spirit of God working for growth in grace, leading the soul into a wider expanse, enlarging the horizon, clearing the outlook, implanting nobler ideals, making "young men to see visions, and old men to dream dreams."

A Vision of Hope

It was in the year 1890 that John Harper got the vision that sealed him for public service. He was at home all alone one Saturday afternoon in the month of June. All around his village home nature was dressed in its best. June is the queen of summer months. The flowers were blooming. The birds were singing. The sun was shining. But while other youths may have been roaming in the green fields, or by babbling brooks, inside that village home the Spirit of God was leading that young lad into green pastures and beside still waters.

An enrapturing vision was given him, almost overpowering in its intensity, in which he saw and felt as never before the purpose of God in the Cross of Christ. In Christ's love for men as seen on Calvary he beheld anew, in fuller form, a door of hope opened for a sinning world, and along with that fresh revelation he felt that God was beckoning to him, and committing to him a part in the ministry of reconciliation. Next day his lips were opened. Taking his stand on the street of his native village he began to pour forth his soul in earnest entreaty for men to be reconciled to God.

A Preacher not Shaped by any University

Any education he had received was obtained at the Board School in his native village, and like many other boys he was not too eager for school lessons. He was anxious to get to work, thinking like others of his age, that work is the mark of manhood. Besides, anything he could earn was needed at home. As soon as he could get away from school his hands were filled with labour. He worked at gardening for a little, but he was at work in a paper mill when he received the fresh anointing, and the call to service.

No university ever got the opportunity of shaping him. He came from God's Hand for service with no college stamp upon him. This may have lessened his status in the eyes of some, but it did not lessen his zeal for the moral and spiritual welfare of his fellow men. And after all it is not what a man acquires in scholarship, but what a man accomplishes in result that counts among right-thinking men.

The Word of God was his Doctrine

He had an orderly mind. This became more noticeable as the years went by, and he was a diligent student of theological works. As a lad he had imbibed a good deal of what is known as Calvinistic doctrine, but of the very rigid, narrow type. However, as he grew in grace and in knowledge, his mind broadened, and he found no difficulty in holding fast any truth or system of doctrine whether termed Calvinistic or Arminian that seemed to have Bible support. Divine Sovereignty and Free Will, as these terms are popularly understood, he embraced and held fast to, believing them to be rooted in the Word of God. How they co-exist he didn't profess to be able to explain, and he didn't argue about them, feeling as the wisest and devoutest of men in all generations have felt that they are matters for faith, and not for discussion.

He was an eager Bible student. He read the Sacred Book. He meditated upon it. He used any commentary that would throw light upon it, or that would help him to draw light from it. He yielded himself to its sway. He expounded it. Few could make better use of it than he "for doctrine, for reproof, for correction, for instruction in righteousness." Whatever form of doctrine was found in it he adhered to. This he did tenaciously. He took fast hold of what instruction it gave him. He esteemed it as his life. Whatever doctrine was not found in the Holy Scriptures, it mattered not how fancifully put, nor by whomsoever it was proclaimed, found no place with him. "Thus saith the Lord" was his stand-by.

He stood on the rock of revelation. Men's theories to him were sand. God's Word was rock. He constantly proved its worth, and he was not ashamed to avow his faith in it. He often quoted texts in an impressive way, and men would remember the text he preached from even if they remembered nothing else.

A gentleman in business in Glasgow remembers seeing him get up in a hall in Kilbarchan about twenty years ago and quote *1st John 1:7*, "The blood of Jesus Christ, God's Son, cleanseth us from all sin." The words "all sin" were repeated by him three times over, each time with growing emphasis. "There's something in that, lad," the gentleman said to himself. Most assuredly there was, and in due season that "something" was seen.

Every Street Corner was his Pulpit

When God is needing a man for His service He knows where to look for him. He scans the field. He sees the need. He chooses the man. He called Elisha from the plough; Amos from the flock; Peter from his fishing boat on the shores of Galilee; and John Harper from the paper mill. And when God puts a man into a berth nobody can give him his "walking ticket." Room will usually be made for him when the gift and calling of God are manifest, and if no room can be made for him in the Church until he is proved and tested and his fitness seen, God will find for him a sphere of service in which to manifest the divine call.

In service for God laborers are always needed, men who are willing to toil and suffer, to spend and be spent, to bear reproach, and endure hardness, as good soldiers of Jesus Christ. John Harper was a labourer—a labourer together with God (I Cor. 3:9), a man who put heart and soul and strength and mind into every bit of service that he rendered. At the outset of his career he dreamed of no church pulpit. If he found an empty street corner when he went anywhere he filled it. That was his pulpit, and he made full use of it. All round about the district where he lived, after receiving the special enduement of power from on high, he went preaching the story of redeeming grace. Bridge-of-Weir, Kilbarchan, Elderslie, Johnstone, Linwood, and else-where would find him at night after his day's work was over, heralding forth with youthful hopefulness the story of God's love to men. His heart was all aglow. He did one thing then, and he did it to the end–he laboured to bring men from sin to God.

This is work that must go on, "The story must be told." Wanderers from God must be followed, warned, pleaded with, and prevailed upon to break with sin and follow Christ. If one of God's servants is taken away, somebody ought to be ready at the divine call to step in and fill the gap. Not necessarily to serve in the same sphere, but to keep alive the same testimony. The number of witnesses must not be thinned down. The world needs the Gospel today as much as ever. The heart of God beats as warmly as ever. The blood of Jesus is as efficacious as ever. The Spirit of God is as much present as ever, yet alas ! it may be that He is so deeply grieved that His power is less in evidence than it would be. There must be work while it is day. This is the day of salvation. The night cometh when no man can work.

"It is a Great Thing to be Sent From God"

After five or six years of earnest, consistent Gospel service, toiling in the mill during the day, and in the rural districts around pleading with men at night to prepare to meet their God, Rev. E. A. Carter of the Baptist Pioneer Mission, London, "discovered" the young village preacher, and set him free to devote his whole time and energy to the work so dear to his heart. Under the auspices of the Mission, a Baptist cause was begun in Govan, one of Glasgow's neighbouring burghs, where there was plenty of elbow room for aggressive work.

For some time mission services were carried on, then a Church was formed. The opening service was conducted by Pastor J. B. Frame, and next day a sermon was preached by Principal MacGregor of Dunoon College, on the words: "There was a man sent from God whose name was John." The text may have provoked a smile, but it was very suitable for the occasion. In that hall there was present a man who beyond all doubt, as after results proved, was sent of God, and his name was John. It is a great thing to be sent from God. The credentials he had with him were the signs that God had already wrought by him. He had no others. But these were sufficient to encourage the belief that God had sent him.

Though young in years he already had a creditable record behind him. The seal of God had been set on his service in the scattered districts where he had witnessed a good confession, and now in the midst of a teeming population it was believed he would be more useful than ever. These hopes were not belied. When God sends a man He supplies all needed grace. No good thing does He withhold from them who walk uprightly in the path of service to which He calls them. Men sent from God with a Gospel message are made the custodians of a power that converts sinners from the error of their way.

But if men run before God sends them, such results will not appear. In Jeremiah's day God made com-plaint through him of those who spoke "a vision out of their own heart, and not out of the mouth of the Lord" *(Jer. 23:16)*. Of them he said: "I have not sent these prophets, yet they ran; I have not spoken to them, yet they prophesied. But if they had stood in my counsel, and had caused my people to hear My words, then they should have turned them from their evil way, and from the evil of their doings" *(Jer. 23:21-22)*. This is a description of un-sent men. Their message is from their own heart. It is not from God. They stand not in God's counsel. They turn none of the people from evil ways, and evil doings.

A God-sent man will speak forth the word of God. Not a vision from his own heart will he declare. The result will be that men will turn from their evil ways, and bow in penitence and adoration at the feet of Him, the once-crucified, but now-glorified Saviour. Under John Harper men turned from their evil ways and evil doings. They forsook uncleanness and followed after holiness without which no man shall see the Lord.

It may have seemed a matter of small moment in the eyes of some, the setting apart of that young man for Gospel ministry that day. But hundreds upon hundreds have reason to bless God that ever they saw his face, or heard his voice. For about eighteen months he toiled incessantly in Govan, plodding, praying, preaching, pleading, touching the hearts and lives of some with his earnest appeals, and gathering about him a small company of men and women who saw in him the marks of a God-sent man.

"Preaching for all he was Worth."

In the early days of his work in Govan one of the members of an evangelistic band was sent as a deputy from the city to speak at a mission service in Govan. When he got to Govan Cross he saw a young man standing there "preaching for all he was worth." "Who is that?" he said to a man who was with him. "That is the Baptist Mission preacher," was the answer. The impression made that night, and deepened afterwards by further acquaintance with the young man who was "preaching for all he was worth," as he has expressed it, led him into fellowship in the Church when it was formed, and made him ever afterwards one of Mr. Harper's staunchest friends.

After a year and a half of service in Govan a move was made to Gordon Halls, Paisley Road. Here on 5th September, 1897, a Church was formed of 25 members, some of whom had come with him from Govan. The Church was named Paisley Road Baptist Church, the name it still bears. But it has been suggested that it should now be called the Harper Memorial Church (and so it is).

Men and women of all ages gathered round the young preacher, and with him as leader, work was carried on in no formal manner. At all the inside meetings increasing effort was made to win men to Christ. Outside, meetings were held at street corners, at the gates of public works at the meal hours, and wherever a hearing could be obtained. The net was cast on every side. The zeal and enthusiasm of the workers seemed boundless. Souls were won, the cause prospered, the membership was increased. The faith which worketh by love and is radiant with hopefulness, animated the workers, and led them on from victory to victory over the forces of unbelief.

After four years in the Gordon Halls, a site was got in Plantation district, and an iron building, capable of seating five or six hundred people, was put up. To it as a centre the work was transferred, and within its walls marvelous things were seen of God's saving power. A continuous stream of pardoning mercy poured itself through the services, and six years ago the building had to be enlarged to make room for the increasing demands of the work. It is situated in the midst of a teeming working-class population. No person living, however closely associated with the work which was carried on can ever know anything fully of the amount of good which was accomplished by Mr. Harper's ministry.

"Yon man, Mr. Harper, was Preaching at the Street Corner, and I Trusted the Lord."

The superintendent of a large evangelistic hall in Glasgow was visiting some time ago an old man in High Street, fully two miles away from Paisley Road Church. The old man, who is in his 80th year, was asked if he was trusting Jesus. At once he answered in the affirmative. On being asked how long it was since he trusted the Saviour, he said, "Nine years." "What age were you, then?" "Just turned 70." "And how did it come about?" "Well, I was passing Plantation, and yon man, Mr. Harper, was preaching at the street corner, and I trusted the Lord there and then." In and around the district in which the Church is situated, there are many, many homes that have been blessed, brightened, beautified, by the preaching of the Lord's servant, whose sad end so many mourn. The Church that was formed with 25 members had a membership of nearly 500 when, after 13 years service, he left in September, 1910, to take up the duties of the pastorate in Walworth Road Church, London. The farewell meeting was a most memorable one. The iron building, seating about 900, was quite inadequate to take in all who desired to attend, and the use of a large U.F. Church in the neighbourhood was kindly granted for the occasion. It was crowded to excess.

A Consuming Earnestness

He was always an earnest preacher. Never a trifler. Never a mere retailer of addresses. He was ever a man who had his gaze fixed on the need of precious souls. But, during the later years of his ministry in Glasgow his preaching seemed to take on a higher note. There was a consuming earnestness that grew with the passing years. His preaching power on occasions was something extraordinary. This was not merely when appealing to the unsaved to be reconciled to God, but also when exhorting the children of God to higher things. Without doubt, as those of us who knew him well can testify, the passionate, vehement longing that found expression in his public utterances had its well-spring in the seasons of pro-longed supplication to which he gave himself. He was pre-eminently a man of prayer.

Barely one month before his end when in Glasgow on a visit he spent half an hour with a few of us over a cup of tea, and the last word we remember him saying was that the need of to-day was a deeper prayer life.

His brief ministry at Walworth Road was very signally blessed of God. Progress was made. The church membership increased. Everything looked hopeful. New ties of interest were formed. New friendships were made. Then came the invitation to conduct special services in the Moody Church in Chicago during the past winter. References to that notable work appear in the later pages of this volume.

When he came back to London in January it was not thought that he would agree to pay a return visit so soon as he arranged to do. But he was going off "early in April," he said to us a fortnight before he sailed. "Why are you going back so early ? Surely not again to conduct special services? . . . Oh, no," he said, "I am going to conduct the regular services in the Moody Church, and speak at conferences and other gatherings elsewhere." Full of hope he set out on the ill-fated steamer, and met his doom on the way. Is that what we should say? Should we not rather say that he met his Lord on the way?

On that fateful Sunday night just an hour or two before the *Titanic* struck the iceberg, he looked at the sky and seeing a glint of red in the west, he said, "It will be beautiful in the morning." Yes, so it would, but the beauty that would break on him was not that which he was alluding to when he spoke these words. The beauty of the Saviour he would see.

After a very brief married life he lost his wife early in the year 1906. Their little daughter, Nina, is now a few months over six years old. The blessing of the Lord will surely rest on the little orphan girl. "A Father of the fatherless . . . is God in His holy habitation" *(Psalm 68:5)*.

Chapter 3

My Brother as I Knew Him
By Pastor George Harper, Edinburgh

To me, Pastor John Harper, who sank with other fifteen-hundred and three persons in the never-to-be-forgotten *Titanic* catastrophe on 15th April, 1912, was my brother in a double sense, in the flesh and in the Lord. Not only so, he was my only brother in the flesh. Together we were brought up, together we bowed at the family altar, as our godly father:

> ". . . Kneeling down to heaven's eternal King;
> The saint, the father, and the husband prayed."

Together we slept as boys in the same room, together we went to school, and together we fished for trout in the little burn that flowed not far from our cottage home. Together we sat in the village church, and with but the brief space of three months between, I may add, together we entered the heavenly pathway, and as the years rolled on we kept step in our beliefs and convictions, in matters spiritual, sharing our joys and sorrows in every possible way. The great ingathering of precious souls into our Lord's Kingdom, which my dear brother witnessed in Chicago last winter, afforded me

Pastor George Harper

The fear of death did not for one moment disturb me. I believed that sudden death would be sudden glory.

John Harper, after nearly
drowning at 32.

unbounded joy. Surely, then, my text will not be grudged me when I quote it, "I am distressed for thee, my brother John; very pleasant hast thou been unto me; thy love to me was wonderful, passing the love of women" (David's words of grief at Jonathan's death, *II Samuel 1:26*).

Saved From Drowning at two Years of Age

The earliest recollection of my boyhood days is associated with an accident that befell my brother. We had been playing some little childish game beside the rather deep spring well at the end of our garden, when John missed his foot and tumbled into the well. He was then only two and a half years old. What could I do? Only one thing, stand at the top of the steps and cry "Mother, mother," for all I was worth. Mother came to the rescue just in time to save John's life.

I well remember how she held his feet up in the air, and how the water flowed from his mouth. I admit it was a somewhat primitive method of resuscitation, but it was mother's method, and it proved to be successful. Nearly drowned at two and a half!

Saved From Drowning at 26 Years of Age

Twenty-four years later we were working together in special mission work as "The Harper Brothers." The day was very fine, we were some miles from Barrow-in-Furness, on the coast. Without considering the possibility of a strong receding tide, we entered the water to bathe. I could swim but a very little, John could not swim one stroke. We were soon in difficulty, but for that Providence which rules all, my brother's life-story might have ended in the sea, and mine too, on that occasion. When once we got safely out of danger, we felt, exhausted though we were, sure that our Heavenly Father had mercifully saved us, and together we praised Him.

Saved From Drowning at 32 Years of Age

Six years after this, when on a trip to Palestine, in company with his personal friend, Mr. Wylie of Glasgow, they were on board a ship on the Mediterranean which sprang a leak. After hours of weary suspense, most of which time they were face to face with death, they were rescued. My brother, in a lecture afterwards graphically described this incident. He said, "The fear of death did not for one moment disturb me. I believed that sudden death would be sudden glory, but, there was a wee motherless girl in Glasgow, and, oh, I thought, if I had only committed her to my dear brother George's care before I left." Needless to say, his brother would unhesitatingly have accepted the trust, whether committed to him or not, a trust he would have considered sacred. Thus on three occasions to my knowledge, prior to the final one on 15th of April, 1912, my brother was face to face with a grave in the waters.

"A Laborious Student"

Our parents were humble people. My father had a drapery business in the village of Houston, which did not yield a very large income, but notwithstanding the problem of bringing up six of a family, he strove to give us all the best possible education. My father was himself a man of fair education, and was widely read. However, John was not mindful in those days, and missed much that would have proved helpful to him in after years, as he often admitted. I think the marvel is that he developed so strikingly. Again and again his diction in address, and in letter-writing was, to me, simply charming. But, from his later teens onward he was a laborious student, few men prepare themselves and their message for the pulpit as he did. This, perhaps is, at least, one explanation of my brother's development.

"He Praised me for Standing up for John"

I well remember our school-master calling John out for punishment. It may have been because of his badly-prepared lessons. I rather think it was. However, the cane was being used somewhat freely and severe. I sat for a short time, then my stronger self asserted itself. In those days, as in all the intervening years, my brother was the apple of my eye. Accordingly I felt within myself, this will not do, lessons or no lessons, this man will not beat my brother after such a fashion. I rose, with my slate in my hand, which I raised above my head, declaring at the same moment, "If you don't stop flogging my brother, I'll do for you." He stopped at once, and came right up to me, and before the whole school praised me for thus standing up for John. Ah! don't you see, John was my brother.

School days were all too soon over, and as stated by others, John went early to work. It was not considered in those days in the country wrong to send a boy to work at the age of fourteen or fifteen. He was supposed to have got a fair education, and to have got some bone. For five years or more he followed various occupations. It was at the beginning of this period in his life that he was led to Christ. I well remember the evening. It was on the last Sunday in March, 1886, that dear John was born of the Spirit. The way had been well prepared for this.

Our Devout Father

My father was a man among men, as my esteemed friend, Mr. Hugh Morris, points out in his tribute. He was a Puritan in theology and in practice, a man who loved his Lord and his Bible. A great admirer of C. H. Spurgeon, whose sermons he constantly read, and that aloud too, and to which, at stated times we had all to listen, whether we enjoyed them or otherwise. Family worship, with the careful reading of the scriptures, and prayer, in conjunction with which we sang together one of David's Psalms, was the order of our cottage home. In this Puritanical atmosphere our family was cradled. John was thus ready in a very real and practical manner for the great event in his life, viz., his surrender to Christ. Mr. Walter B. Sloan, and Mr. Archibald Orr Ewing, both now of the China Inland Mission, occupied the village Free Church pulpit that evening. My dear brother sat beside me in our family pew.

"We Became one in the Faith"

At the close of the service an after-meeting was held, John, with others, waited behind, and from John 3:16 was led to see God's rich provision in Jesus for his salvation. Three months before I had accepted Christ. as my personal Saviour. Now we were one in the faith that is in Christ Jesus. Yes, and thank God, this oneness in spiritual fellowship was never broken throughout the twenty-six years of our Christian companionship. I well remember how my beloved father rejoiced when he realized that God had answered his prayers in the conversion to Christ of his two boys, to be followed shortly after with the additional assurance that some of his daughters too had embraced Christ.

My brother's subsequent life story is largely told in this book by others, the further revelation and call he received in the year 1890, his going forth with whole-hearted zeal into his Lord's work in the village of Houston (his Jerusalem), and the surrounding villages. Suffice it, therefore, that I give only a few of the inner sidelights of his Christian character and work. In the course of time the Houston village mission, described so well on another page by Mr. Hugh Morris, came to an end. This mission, commenced by Mr. W. B. Sloan, in the summer of 1885, continued for some years. In the early nineties it was stopped. I was then from home in business, and only returned once every fortnight. My brother, with a few others, conducted open-air meetings every Sunday afternoon. When at home I gladly assisted.

On one such occasion a big man who had repeatedly declared his intention of stopping these meetings, came upon the scene. Alas for us on this occasion, we numbered only two persons–my brother and myself. We sang a duet, then took our turn at preaching. The man would have none of it. He was six feet two or three inches in height, and powerfully built. He shook his fist in our faces, and threatened to deform us if we persisted in preaching, but my brother's indomitable spirit was in no way scared, we continued to preach and sing for Jesus, despite his threats. After a time he left us, and in peace we continued and concluded that somewhat eventful open-air meeting.

The work in the Gryffe Grove Hall, Bridge-of-Weir, and in Johnstone, and other neighbouring towns, with which my dear brother was so closely identified would require a volume by itself to do it justice. These were years of burning zeal for Christ and His Kingdom. Many were led to Christ through my brother's faithful gospel ministry, and God's people were quickened and revived. I had the unspeakable joy of assisting him, as opportunity afforded, in these early years, and saw much of the inner side of his life, which was transparently clean and true. I gladly bear witness to this. I will not detail the story of how John was led to enter the Baptist ministry. This period in his life had three distinct chapters, viz., Govan, Paisley Road, Glasgow, and Walworth Road, London. In each sphere God's hand was distinctly laid upon His servant in power. But especially was this the case in Paisley Road, Glasgow.

"Mighty in Prayer"

During his thirteen years' ministry there, hundreds upon hundreds were swept into Christ's Kingdom. Let me once more take you to the inner side of all this. Others will tell you the story from the outside. My beloved brother was a man mighty in prayer. He was a master in this holy art.

In October, 1899, I came from Bradford, where I was then Pastor, to Paisley Road, to conduct a month's mission. Night after night, just as I was about to announce my text, John would slip off the platform into a small side vestry, and fall upon his knees in prayer. There he would wrestle with God, as I pled with men. Needless to say the results of that mission abide today. I have been with my dear brother in prayer, again and again, when his whole frame shook like an aspen leaf, so earnest was he in his pleadings with God for a perishing world. He often wept. in prayer. Like his Lord he offered up his supplications with "strong crying and tears" *(Heb. 5:7)*. Little wonder hard hearts were broken, and stubborn wills subdued under his ministry.

As I listened to him in prayer I used to say, "Dear John is far ben" ("ben" meant "the innermost, the intimate part of the house" in 19th Century Scotland). He seemed to live on the most intimate terms with his Lord. There was nothing mawkish about his piety. He never tried to make one feel that he was holier than others, yet one instinctively felt that he was a man of God, whose supreme joy was in fellowship with his Lord and Redeemer.

Sorrows Shaped his Life

The full story of those thirteen years of consecrated Christian labour will never be told. To my beloved brother they were years of joy and sorrow. Every convert did not turn out to be a "crown of rejoicing" unto the Lord's servant. The weak and faltering ones caused my brother much pain, and backsliders nearly broke his heart. But the joys of this period more than counterbalanced its sorrows. Many sought and found Christ, and ever after followed on to know the Lord. It was during this time that two great sorrows befell my brother.

In the summer of 1905 his health broke down, his voice, which was in the early days, rich and resonant, completely failed him. For six months he was unfit for duty. This was a very severe trial to him. He wept with me and I with him over this trial. However, a sea voyage and a complete rest, with special treatment, in due time brought back, at least, partial strength and energy to him. But he was never the same in physical fitness afterwards. Those who only knew him during his closing years saw but the skeleton of the former days, that is, in the physical power and mighty appeal.

True, during the last five or six years of his life there was a wonderful mellowing, a ripening, that those of us who were in the more intimate fellowship did not fail to perceive. We saw the outer man waxing weaker, and the inner man stronger every time we met.

"Annie is Dying"

But a greater sorrow still lay across his path. Early in 1906 his wife was taken from him. Mrs. Harper was a real help-meet to him. She was some years his senior, and was of a bright disposition. My brother and she, then Miss Bell, met during the Bridge-of-Weir mission work. For ten years they waited for each other. I greatly rejoiced in my brother's marriage with Miss Bell. But, alas! their married life was of short duration. It covered little more than two years. A little girl was born at New-year, 1906, and not many days later Mrs. Harper's spirit "winged its flight to realms of day."

I will never forget that event. I was then Pastor of Bellshill Baptist Church. It was Sunday evening, I had just given out my text, *Isaiah 28:15-18*, "A covenant with death," when I was called into the vestry, a policeman wanted to see me. He had received a message by wire from my brother. It read as follows, "Dear George, please come at once, Annie is dying. I want Mary and you beside me." The Mary here mentioned was my own wife.

I returned to my service, called two of our office-bearers on to the platform, and left the service in their hands. A cab was hired, and with all speed my wife and myself got to my beloved brother's side in his deep sorrow. Ah, he was my brother, and nothing would have kept me from him in his trial. We stood by Mrs. Harper's bed for twelve hours doing all in our power to comfort her, and alleviate her pain, and then, when her spirit entered the brighter home above, we gently closed her eyelids.

This trial, coming as it did upon the one through which he passed the year before, completely prostrated him. It was his Gethsemane, his fiery baptism. The cup was a bitter one, but he drank it, meanwhile saying, "Not my will, but Thine be done."

Caring for his Baby Daughter

Shortly after this, my dear wife prevailed upon him to allow us to keep wee Nana for him, which he did for about six months. We would gladly have kept the little pet all through the years that have followed for her father's sake, and for her own sake, but that joy was not granted us. My brother sadly missed the fellowship of his dear wife. His home was never the same to him after. He had a nature that craved for companionship. Only a few months before he was taken from us we were together for some days. It was like new life to him. We prayed, sang, walked, and talked much together. How he poured into my ear matters that touched his future, assuring me that to no other one had he thus opened his mind. Would that it had been God's will to have spared him to have carried through some of these plans and purposes.

The Move to London

When he accepted the invitation to the pastorate of the Church in Walworth Road, London, he wrote to me telling about his anticipated farewell services in Paisley Road. I was urgently requested by him to come to his farewell tea meeting. This I did ungrudgingly. I had been at his first induction service in Govan, and I sat, by his special request, at his side on this last occasion. What a meeting it was. Tears were shed and tributes paid to his sterling worth, but not one sentence in my hearing was exaggerated. In London, as in Glasgow, God set his seal on His servant's work.

In one year the old Church, with many worthy traditions attached to its history, passed through a remarkable season of reviving grace. It bids fair, under the ministry of my esteemed friend and brother, Pastor A. Moncur Nibtock, who was co-pastor with dear John, to rival Paisley Road. This was my conviction during a recent visit I paid to it. Then Chicago!

Chicago Mourns Harper's Passing

Who can speak of the marvelous work accomplished through the instrumentality of my precious brother in the famous Moody Church in that city during the winter months of 1911-1912? Rev. E. Y. Woolley, assistant Pastor of that great Church, in a letter to me on 11th May, says, "I have returned to Chicago to find, as I expected, our people grief-stricken through the loss of Mr. Harper. Our mid-week meeting last night was crowded to the doors. We had fully three hundred more people than usually attend, and hundreds were weeping as the meager details of his passing were told. I never knew a man who had so gripped the hearts of people in three short months of fellowship. Next Sunday morning is to be given to a memorial service for him, but it is easy to see that everyone of our meetings will be to a large extent memorials. God used him while here as I never have seen a man used before." Such is Mr. Woolley's testimony.

I possess a number of letters written to me by dear John from Chicago. The one vehement desire expressed in all these letters is that I would pray for him. "Pray for me, pray for me every minute," thus he wrote. My brother never spared himself, but as the years advanced he seemed to sacrifice himself more and more for others, and specially for his Lord.

Reaping in Chicago

The Life of Faith, referring to this wonderful work of grace in Chicago, says, "His services were attended with such rich blessing that the visit lengthened into three months, the

Moody Church passing through one of the most wonderful revivals in its history. The Lord's own people also received a spiritual uplift, a practical illustration of which was seen in the fact that a debt of L1,000 was wiped out in four days."

On his return from Chicago he paid a brief visit to Scotland, coming first to Edinburgh where he addressed two meetings, both being held in our Church at Gorgie. His word was with great power. From Edinburgh he traveled to Glasgow, then to Paisley, Denny, and Cumnock in Ayrshire. In all these places his ministry was "in the Holy Ghost and in much assurance," though he was considerably run down in body.

The Call to Return to Chicago

At the urgent and most cordial request of the Moody Church in Chicago he consented to return for three months more. In a letter to me dated London, 1st April, he wrote, "We are sailing on Saturday with the *Lusitania* from Liverpool." Would God he had gone by that boat instead of by the ill-fated *Titanic* a week later.

The *Titanic* sailed from Southampton for New York on the 10th of April. On the 15th of April she went down into the bosom of the ocean, carrying with her 1522 precious lives, and amongst these my own beloved brother and companion, John Harper.

The details of this sad disaster need not be re-told by me here; they are known to everybody, I suppose, in our land, more or less, and I dare say the generation after the present one will be familiar with this dreadful catastrophe at sea, in calm weather, when the acme of man's genius in mercantile shipbuilding on her maiden voyage perished. I cannot attempt to explain the Providence that removes such a man of God in the midst of his usefulness.

Harper's "Abundant Entrance"

I can only say my confidence is in the over-ruling wisdom of God. "Some day we'll understand." I think Keble puts it well when he writes :

> "Thy God hath said 'tis good for thee
> To walk by faith and not by sight,'
> Take it on trust a little while;
> Soon shalt thou read the mystery right,
> In the bright sunshine of His smile."

One truly feels this is all one can do in the presence of such Providence. There was no farewell message sent to us from the sinking ship, not even a parting kiss, so far as we know, given to his little child. Calm and collected he handed her to one of the ship's officials on the top deck, whilst he himself remained by orders of the captain on the second deck. This was only half an hour before the mighty leviathan took her final plunge.

What his thoughts were during that last half hour on earth, no one will ever tell. One thing we rest assured of, there was "no moaning at the bar" when he "put out to sea." His was "the abundant entrance:"

> "E'en for the dead,
> I will not bind my soul to grief.
> As though death can divide:
> For is it not as though
> the rose that climbed my garden wall,
> Had blossomed on the other side?
> Death doth hide
> But not divide
> Thou art but on the other side,
> Thou art with Christ and Christ with me,
> In Christ united still are we."

"Think More of the Life That is,
Than of the Life That was."

Along with scores of others an esteemed brother writes to me, "Do not grudge the liberty your Heavenly Father has taken with you. He has honoured you, and at the same time fulfilled his own promise, 'where I am there shall also my servant be.' The angels would have a warm welcome for your brother. Think more of the life that is, than of the life that was. More of the abundant entrance, than of the strange, sudden departure. Love and wisdom are on the throne–perfect love and perfect wisdom. It may seem at times all so strange, but it must be right. Try and dig a well in your Valley of Baca."

Thanks, dear brother, this is what I have been trying to do, and as my well becomes deeper, my soul longs yet more and more for the glorious coming morn when the enigmas of life will be read in "His light clearly."

I would like to say here how deeply I value all the kind messages of sympathy that I have received in this my hour of sorrow and weeping. Will friends please accept of this assurance of my personal appreciation? I am not alone in my sorrow. My dear wife has been broken-hearted over the loss of her brother-in-law. Then my sisters—Mrs. Sinclair and Mrs. Given in Johnstone, Mrs. Balloch in St. Boswell's, and Mrs. Auckland in Govan, all weep with me over our irreparable loss. Our brother was very dear to us as a family. To one and all of us his "love was wonderful," and by us (sisters and brother) it was reciprocated.

Oh, That His Soul—ravishing Voice
Would so Reach our Cold Hearts"

His little girl, Nina, does not realize her great loss yet. May her father's God put his mantle over her and protect her from the blast of a cold, sinful world! May our Heavenly Father's will concerning her be carried out, and in some measure at least, her earthly father's spirit of devotion to his Lord in due time be found in her.

Multitudes sorrow over the loss of my beloved brother. He was a great soul-winner, and a true pastor. He led multitudes to the feet of Christ, and afterwards fed them upon the finest of the wheat. His analytic and homiletic gifts were of a very high order, as will be seen in another part of this book, and as other brethren gladly bear witness to this fact I merely mention it.

In a letter to one of his sisters, as far back as 27th of June, 1892, when he was a young preacher, he wrote, "Oh that we could only have more faith in a loving, living Saviour, and that we would only open our hearts wide enough to receive more of His sweet, consuming, constraining, heart-piercing love, and oh! that we would open our ears to hear the sweet voice of the Bridegroom as He whispers to our souls, `Arise, my love, my fair one, and come away, and leave the fleeting phantoms of this fleeting day.' And oh, that His soul-ravishing voice would so reach our cold hearts that we would be made to thirst and cry out for a closer fellowship with the crucified Saviour."

Such is only a brief quotation from a letter in front of me, many parts of which one feels are too sacred for public print. Ah, yes ! the message of the Cross was the message of his burning ministry from first to last. But perhaps in a very special degree the Cross filled his vision during his closing ministry. His intention was to write and publish in book form some of these addresses which God used in the Chicago movement, but God saw fit to write them in another way, indelibly upon the hearts and lives of ransomed sinners and revived saints. Some hundreds of his rich and suggestive outlines are buried in an ocean grave. Nevertheless of his witness and work for his Lord we can truly say, "He being dead yet speaketh."

My Brother's Weakness

There was a side of my brother's character which seemed somewhat out of harmony with the side I have written at length upon. He was very easily imposed upon. I often remonstrated with him regarding this. I could easily give instance after instance from my own personal knowledge of how he suffered, and sometimes severely and for long, at the hands of those who were little short of impostors. But he would only reply when remonstrated with, "Well, well, the Lord knows about them, He will deal with them." But for this little weakness in his character, to some of us who knew him intimately, he would have been little short of our ideal in human perfection.

The reader will please be assured that I seek in all I write concerning my beloved brother to magnify the grace of Christ as so wonderfully manifested in His servant. I feel this poor, groaning, dying world, steeped in sin, and openly rejecting Christ, can ill afford to part with a man of Goal like my brother, who constantly wept over it, and poured out his life's strength for it. I also feel the Church of Christ, alas, so often lethargic, can ill afford to bid adieu to a ministry so awakening, so needful. But it may be God in this way is calling to deeper consecration, to truer service, to the filling of the breach made by dear John's translation, some others of His servants. "Whilst Thou'rt calling, Lord, call me." May multitudes be baptized with the same spirit and zeal and enthusiasm for the glory of Christ, the conversion of the lost, and the hastening of the day of the long looked-for coming of our Lord and Saviour Jesus Christ.

Chapter 4

He Rose From The Ranks Of The Working Men

Tribute by Pastor John Dick,
Paisley Road Baptist Church, Glasgow

To write an appreciation of John Harper is no easy task; for when one has written in the superlative degree, one feels that justice has not been done to the life-work and character of this strenuous worker for God.

I knew Mr. Harper for twelve years, and seven years ago, I spent ten days with him while conducting a special mission in Paisley Road. Then I learned to love him, and to know John Harper better was to love him more. We were different men, but there was an affinity between us that strengthened with the years, and his great desire was that I should succeed him-in Paisley Road, if ever he should be led out of it. That is now an accomplished fact; but little did we think that his earthly race would be completed at thirty-nine.

Pastor John Dick

Reclaimed drunkards,
gamblers, prize fighters,
now enthusiastic workers for God,
all praise the Saviour whom they love
for the day they came
into touch with John Harper.

He was a Man Taught of God

In losing our dear brother, we have lost a great preacher. Stepping out from the ranks of the working men, he stood before his fellows as a man taught of God. No college can claim him; he came forth a preacher from God. The passion of his life was soul-winning. It was no unusual thing for him never to go to bed on a Saturday night, pleading for souls, and crying for Divine Power to enable him to preach for the glory of God. It was this passionate love for souls that made him literally live among the people.

Harper won the Hearts of the Common people

With pride the people in the district tell me how he used to drop in to dinner or tea, and sit down with them to their frugal meal, served on a table devoid of cloth. He was one of themselves, losing himself in their sorrows and joys— advising and warning, rejoicing and weeping—and in this manly, loving way he endeared himself to the simple people who today mourn his loss as if he had been one of their own family.

His love and sympathy were phenomenal, because of the magnetic sympathetic influence that ever emanated from him. No wonder Roman Catholic and Protestant, the poor and the poorest of the poor, shed copious tears at the mention of his death! The district loved him and appreciated the Herculean efforts of this great, passion-ate worker for God.

Lives Were Forever Changed

He was a great Bible student, and his capable teaching is manifest in the numbers of young men in the congregation who have an intelligent grasp of the Book of Books, and who have caught Pastor Harper's enthusiasm for Bible study. In Paisley Road and Walworth Road, London, his magnificent grasp of Bible truths was instrumental in bringing back many to the main line who had gone off to side tracks. One man in a prominent position in London told the writer that he owed his present position to John Harper who had convinced him of doctrinal error by his intelligent exposition of the Living Word. Another prominent worker for God says, that but for John Harper he would to-day have been wandering in the mazes of infidelity.

Reclaimed drunkards, gamblers, prize fighters, now enthusiastic workers for God, all praise the Saviour whom they love for the day they came into touch with John Harper. Personal dealing was his great forte, his tact and greatness of soul eminently fitting him for this work.

He knew working-men's difficulties and temptations; he knew their literature and their manner of thinking; because he was one of them, and while some of them might resent what they called his extreme attitude, yet they loved him and were the first to recognize his intense sincerity.

He was a great open-air preacher, and could always Command large and appreciative audiences. People speak with pride of the effect of his magnificent voice in the open-air, and tell how cleverly and firmly he could deal with all kinds of interrupters. No one could "floor" him, his great and intelligent grasp of Bible truths enabling him to successfully combat all assailants.

It was a very common sight to see souls being dealt with in the open-air, some even kneeling down in the ring and making confession of sin. Some of these trophies of grace are to-day deacons and respected members of Paisley Road Baptist Church, which is built on the spot where many of its members once gambled and fought! What a testimony to the power of the Gospel, working through a man completely abandoned to the great work of soul-winning!

An Inspiration to Thousands

What a sermon builder he was! His homiletical ability was marvelous. His great doctrinal sermons grew under his treatment until they appeared like a magnificent branching tree, affording shade and shelter to many a weary traveler. His wide knowledge of Puritan, Theological and Revival literature enabled him to embellish his discourses in such a way as to send the hearer away with a sense of satisfaction and fullness.

How difficult it is for one to realize that this great, intelligent, earnest, enthusiastic preacher and soul winner has gone out of one's life! All denominations mourn his loss, for his energies were freely given to all, as he didn't know the meaning of ministerial jealousy. His life will be an inspiration to thousands, his influence will be indelible, his example infectious, and although he was struck down in the zenith of his usefulness, yet we do not grudge him his translation to higher service. To try to fill his place is to attempt the impossible, yet to be in his place is an inspiration.

He has gone to his reward, and it is for those who knew and loved him to profit by his example and try to fill the gap as far as is possible.

Farewell, my beloved brother! May your mantle as a preacher, fall upon your unworthy successor, and may the passion that filled your soul control the writer of this inadequate at appreciation.

Chapter 5

"He Could Not Live Without Souls Being Won"

Tribute by Pastor Hugh Gunn,
John Street Baptist Church, Glasgow

Our dear brother, Mr. Harper, was a man in Christ. He was wholly surrendered to God. I knew him well, and I never saw in him anything to the contrary. He had no hobby, and sought no recreation other than the deepening of his delight in God. Every power and passion of his being seemed to thrill with the life of God. He was on the altar continually.

A Passion for Holiness

He was a man of intense earnestness. This earnestness was begotten of his consciousness of God. The power of the world to come seemed to rest on him at all times. This characterized him continually, whether praying, preaching, or dealing personally with individuals regarding salvation.

He was a man of prayer. I shall never forget seasons of prayer with him. He no sooner began praying audibly than every one felt he was in touch with God. After hearing him

Pastor Hugh Gunn

*Would he not in the midst of
that sweltering mass of
drowning men, women and children
be pointing them to the Cross,
and thus as he lived, die with that one
name upon his lips—
Jesus ! Jesus ! ! Jesus ! ! ! ?*

pray, one felt the desire to go away alone and open out one's heart before God. Prayer took a great deal out of him. He laboured in prayer, praying in the Holy Ghost. It was quite a common thing for him to spend whole nights alone in prayer. He literally came from the presence of God to his people. His sermons were saturated with prayer. Hence their great power in uplifting and sanctifying God's people, and bringing sinners weeping to the Cross.

God's Hand Rested Upon him

He was a man of God. A holy man of God. God was all in all to him. He was always in communion with God. He reveled in the precariousness of Christ. God's hand of power rested upon him. This undoubtedly was the secret of his constant possession of that indescribable, indefinable thing we call unction. I never heard him speak without it.

As A Pastor, he was most careful in his preparation for the pulpit. He reminded one of M'Cheyne's saying, "beaten oil for the sanctuary." Saint and sinner seemed to be thoroughly understood by him, and each had their portion dealt out to them as in the sight of God. With what eagerness he sought to lead God's people into the fullness of the blessed life in Christ, dreading their remaining satisfied with anything short of the abundant, overflowing life which filled his own soul. He was greatly blessed in leading Christians out into the service of Christ. He never urged them to be or do that which he was not or did. He led the way.

His passion for souls

Our beloved brother possessed a consuming zeal for souls. This was really the outstanding feature of his consecrated life. He seemed to be unable to live without souls being won to Christ. Souls! Souls! ! Souls! ! ! colored his whole life.

He was loyal to God's Word. He never descended into the questionable paths of higher criticism. To him it was God's Word.

He was most intolerant with regard to some of the modern methods of doing Christian work. To him it was little short of blasphemy to offer dying men entertainments and amusements instead of the glorious Gospel which bringeth salvation to all men. His own work was a living example of what the Gospel alone can accomplish.

"Come up Higher"

Being greatly blessed to the Moody Church, Chicago, he was invited to return for a second mission, and on his way there Christ came to him and said, "Come up higher." What a meeting with his Lord! I am intensely curious to know how he acted in the closing moments of his life. Would he not, as was his wont, be drying the tear away, comforting, and helping till the last moment of his life? Would he not in the midst of that sweltering mass of drowning men, women and children be pointing them to the Cross, and thus as he lived, die with that one name upon his lips—Jesus! Jesus! ! Jesus! ! ! ?

Chapter 6

There Will Never Be Another

Tribute by Pastor A. M. Niblock, Delivered at Walworth Road Baptist Church, London

It is with indescribable feelings that I stand here this morning. The great calamity which has fallen upon us, in the loss of our beloved pastor, the Rev. John Harper, has plunged us into a pathless darkness from which for the moment our hearts and minds cannot find a way out. Last Monday evening we went from the prayer meeting to our homes full of praise to God for the preservation of our beloved friend.

The Failed Promise of an Unsinkable Ship

The news-papers told us he was upon an unsinkable ship, that all was safe, and therefore there was no need to fear, but alas! man's word is not like God's word—immutable, unchanging and sure. Neither are man's works like God's, for both words and works have failed, as has been seen in this sad disaster. The ship was sinkable and she sank, and with her went down into the dark deep the body of him whom we

Pastor A. Moncur Niblock

There was only one John Harper,
and there will never be another,
no one will ever fill his place.
He has gone; we are left, left ! for what?
To weep and allow
our hands to hang down?
No, surely no!
but to work, to watch, to wait,
to preach Christ and Him crucified,
and thus to save those who are crying out
to us, "Save our souls."

loved so well, but, praise God, we know he himself has gone home to be with the Lord.

We have suffered a great loss, and not only we, but the entire Church of God, a loss which cannot be replaced. There was only one John Harper, and there will never be another, no one will ever fill his place. He has gone; we are left, left ! for what ? To weep and allow our hands to hang down ? No, surely no ! but to work, to watch, to wait, to preach Christ and Him crucified, and thus to save those who are crying out to us, "Save our souls."

My heart sympathizes with yours, yes, we are suffering together, and God only knows the extent of the void that is in your hearts this morning.

Our Furnace of Affliction

God loves this Church, He honoured it by giving for a season, this man of prayer, to lead it into the green pastures of truth, and to the quiet waters of communion with God. The very fact that he was found here proves the love of God for you, and that God has chosen this people for Himself, that He might show forth His glory and virtue through you. Today you are in the furnace of affliction. But is that not where God chooses His people? Isaiah says, "I have chosen you in the furnace of affliction," and so in this which has come upon us, God is choosing us for Himself.

England to-day is a land of mourning. There are many widows and orphans who, but a short time ago were counting the days, yea hours, when they would have the joy of meeting their loved ones again. To-day their hearts are crushed. Desolation has entered into their spirits, and they are lonely, their future is dark, and the spirit of the companionless has taken hold of them. Now they have no one to lean upon, to look up to, to commune with, their partner has gone, that one who was their other being, that one in whom they had lost themselves, and of whom they themselves were a part.

"He Prayed for you. How he Prayed."

God help us then to play the part of the true Christian and remember these in our prayers, before the eternal throne. I have said that we have lost a friend, a brother and a pastor. This is true, is it not? He was a friend indeed. We could go to him and open our hearts, knowing that he would hold sacred our confidence, that he would be gentle with us, and deal with us tenderly, and that whatever advice he gave could be relied upon.

Then he was a pastor, a shepherd. It was borne in upon you that he was a man who realized that he had to render an account to the great Shepherd of the flock over which he had the oversight.

He prayed for you. How he prayed! Some few of us had the privilege of spending seasons together with him in waiting upon God, and at these times he would lose himself entirely, often have we been amazed at his boldness, asking God for great things, and speaking to Him as if he were well acquainted with him. I have never met any man who was his equal in wrestling with God. I have seen the sweat literally pour from him as he agonized in prayer.

At times he seemed to have taken eagle wings to himself and be far away from us, far away in that blue sky where God is, and yet at the same time we realized that he brought heaven down to earth. When John Harper prayed, heaven and earth met, and those near him knew it, because they felt it.

He was a Brainerd, an Edwards, a M'Cheyne, a William Burns, a Finney, and a Caughey rolled into one. How he prayed for the lambs of the flock! O friends, we owe a great debt to our Lord Jesus for allowing him to enter into our life. We are spiritually richer today because of his prayers, and in days to come when spiritual blessings fall upon us, remember that in a great measure many of them will be the answers to our departed brother's prayers.

He Lived Virtually Homeless and Died Without a Grave

Our friend, brother, and pastor has gone home. When his dear wife was taken from him some six years ago, he was, in a sense, a homeless man. It was his wife that made that home, just a little outside Glasgow, "home" to him. Now he has gone to her, and yet far better than even this, he has gone to his Lord and Saviour, whom he adored, loved and served.

When the *Titanic* went down it took with it his poor frail body, but not his spirit, for that has gone home to God. We must not, therefore, think of him as we knew him after the flesh, but as he is now with Christ. If we think of the man after the flesh, we shall see the poor body down in the sea, and imagine that he is cold and lonely, which is not so. No, friends, we sorrow not as others. That body was but the earthly dwelling place of a noble man of God. The man has gone, and the earthly tabernacle is now tenantless. We would if we could, cover and guard, and lovingly lay that body in the grave, because of the soul that once lived in it, but we cannot, and we, therefore, submit and bow to the will of God. For God has been pleased to take our brother to Himself in this manner, for what purpose we do not know, but one thing we do know, God has done right, and to His will we say, Amen!

Chapter 7

"The Melting Earnestness And Intensity of the Man"

Tribute by Mr. Hugh Morris, Evangelist

It was my privilege to have the friendship of Mr. John Harper for twenty-five years, and on reading the news of his sad end from the newspapers, after the awful Titanic disaster, could scarcely credit that such could be the fate of one I had parted with but a short time before, who, never since I had known him, seemed more fit for work physically, intellectually and spiritually. I had heard him preach frequently, but the address he gave at the Noon Meeting in Bothwell Street, Glasgow, on the day of our last meeting on earth, Wednesday, 20th March, stamped itself upon my mind by its lucidity, earnestness and spiritual power, making one feel sure that his gifts as a proclaimer of God's good news were not spent, but had increased and strengthened since I had previously been in his company.

Twenty-five years ago he began as a boy of fully fourteen years of age to work in the gardens of Barrochan House, Houston, Renfrewshire. Of sallow complexion and fragile

Mr. Hugh Morris, Evangelist

*Of sallow complexion and fragile frame,
he did not look very strong:
No one could have anticipated that
he would have lived through those years
to perform the great work he did,
for as a worker in the Master's vineyard
he laboured incessantly, as all know
who came into contact with him.*

frame, he did not look very strong: No one could have anticipated that he would have lived through those years to perform the great work he did, for as a worker in the Master's vineyard he laboured incessantly, as all know who came into contact with him. One marked feature of those early years that made radiant his young life was his reverence for the things of God.

It was my good fortune to know John's parents, and who can over-estimate the benign influence of a home where Christ is Lord and Master, upon the young life growing up in the midst? His father was a most unassuming man, yet withal a man who made himself felt, for the love of God that filled his heart made him think, speak and act in such a manner as to declare with no uncertain voice that he was a "servant of Jesus Christ" as the following incident will show.

John Harper Could Handle Ridicule

One day in a farmyard, the workers were putting up hay in stacks, the farmer, started to taunt him and sneer at his religion as he passed by. The workers laughed. George Harper said nothing for a time, but afterwards turning on him he repeated *Rev. 21:8* ("But the fearful, and unbelieving, and the abominable, and murderers, and whoremongers, and sorcerers, and idolaters, and all liars, shall have their part in the lake which burneth with fire and brimstone: which is the second death.") and some other texts of a kindred nature.

The laughter ceased, the old farmer stood trembling, then turning on his heel fled into the house. From that day on no one on that farm ever attempted to make light of George Harper or his religion. A man of true piety, mighty in the Scripture and powerful in prayer. Many a day at the meal hour I have sat with my Bible in hand and listened with great profit to this "Master in Israel" opening up the Scripture. No one could listen to him as he prayed and not be moved by the melting earnestness and intensity of the man. One could never doubt but that he knew the straight road to the throne of grace.

I had left that district and gone home to reside at Largs. John Harper had gone to work in the carpet work at Elderslie, later on in the paper mill at Kilbarchan. The call came to preach the Gospel, and he obeyed. All round that district, Johnstone, Kilbarchan, Linwood, Elderslie, and Bridge-of-Weir he went preaching with power. First the School House and then a hall was taken for meetings in Bridge-of-Weir. I was asked several times to spend a week-end there.

There are Five Here who
Have not yet Decided for Christ

One meeting lives in my memory. The Sabbath day was wet and stormy. At the hour of meeting at night the weather had not improved. We were looking for a small gathering, as the way leading to the hall was down a long, dark, somewhat circuitous lane lined with trees. When on the platform, after he had given out the hymn, I asked him if he thought there were any unsaved present. He knew the workers well, and after a minute he whispered to me, "There are five here who have not yet decided for Christ." I asked him to pray for the conversion of these five, and I would preach for their conversion. "Agreed," he said, with a smile. When the first meeting was over no one made to go away. No pressure was brought to bear upon any, nor stratagems used to trap them. All voluntarily sat still, and on the five being asked if they desired to trust Christ they said they did, and all five made profession of faith in Jesus before leaving the hall. He used to speak of this meeting when we met in after days.

At 20 Years of age he was the Leading Spirit

Another gathering he organized was an open-air conference for Christian workers on the Brae of Ranfurly, Bridge-of-Weir, on a Saturday afternoon in the summer-time. I took part in giving an address at that conference, and can remember still the large gathering and the healthy spiritual life displayed by all present.

When one calls to mind that at this time he was not quite 20 years of age, and yet the leading spirit in all this work, it shows us that, coupled with those succeeding years of arduous toil and unfading zeal for the winning of the lost for Christ, he was not laboring in energy of the flesh, but in the "power of the spirit," having received orders from "the Leader and Commander" to go forth.

Of him it can be said now that his day's work is over, having put "his hand to the plough" he never looked back. About the time when he was carrying on work in full swing in the above-mentioned district, he wrote to me saying he saw, and was convinced from the Word of God that he should be baptized by immersion, also requesting me to perform the rite.

I was not a pastor, nor at that time had even the title of "evangelist," but as he was insistent that I should baptize him, one Sabbath morning we went together to the Noddle Burn on the north side of Largs, and there, in the pool under the bridge on the Wemyss Bay road, John Harper, in obedience to his Lord, was baptized in New Testament form.

The Last Words of John and his Father to me

The last time I saw his godly father in life we had a talk together of the "things concerning the King." And though at that time he was going about following his daily occupation, most calmly and with emphasis he assured me that he knew he was near the end of his sojourn here. In health, he was his usual, but he told me the prayers of many years had been answered, and the home call would come soon. True it was, for ere two weeks had passed I was in Houston at his funeral.

Towards the end of last March I shook hands with John. He was going oft shortly afterwards to Chicago. He said, "I may see you out there yet." "Yes, keep believing," was my rejoinder. No. Not Chicago, but "the City which hath foundation," where no Gospel campaigns are carried on, no sin, no partings, no heart-rending catastrophes, no blinding grief's. With Christ, with Him for ever, we shall meet, bless God.

Chapter 8

A Brave Soldier on Flame For God

Tribute by Mr. W. D. Dunn,
Evangelist

I gladly contribute my affectionate testimony to the fidelity and sterling worth of the late Pastor John Harper. I knew him for over twenty years, and during all that period we were in the closest fellowship with each other, in seeking the sanctification of the saints of God, and the salvation of perishing souls. During my long experience in Christian work I have been in touch with the cream of the Lord's dear workmen, and without reserve, I can say that no pastor, nor teacher, nor evangelist ever moved my inner being more than the pleading and preaching of Pastor John Harper did; as he was always on flame for God and souls.

"Give me Souls or I die"

John Welch, in the corner of his glebe (meadow), at the mid-night hour, said, "Oh God, give me Scotland, or I die;" and how often I have heard Pastor Harper say, when lying on

Mr. W.D. Dunn, Evangelist

*And now the brave soldier's
precious form
lies beneath the ocean waves,
and his blood-washed spirit
is present with the Lord
in yon land of light and glory,
the homeland of all who love and
serve the Christ of God.
Farewell, beloved soldier,
we shall meet you in the morning
without a cloud.*

his face before God, covered with perspiration, "Oh God, give me souls, or I die." Then he would sob and weep, as if his heart would break. Can we wonder that God gave him souls for Christ, in hundreds?

Our beloved brother was a deep student of the precious Word of God–he believed it was God-breathed from Genesis to Revelation; and he preached it with a clear vision. I have often seen his after-meetings in Paisley Road Baptist Church more like a battlefield than anything else; saints sobbing on account of their unlikeness to Christ, and poor lost sinners crying out for salvation.

Harper "Lived Next Door to Heaven"

What glorious triumphs of grace were won through his Holy-Ghost ministry in that part of the city! And wherever he went, whether in public or in private, he carried with him the holy fragrance of his Lord. I often felt, after being with him in the Gospel or at our Royal Lord's Court, that he was fast ripening for higher service. He lived next door to heaven, hence his soul was constantly inhaling heaven's atmosphere.

The blessing of soul our brother enjoyed saved him from every vestige of sectarianism; so that he preached in perfect harmony with all the other sections of the Christian Church. He had learned through grace that the Church and the work of the Church are one, and he was ready to lend a helping hand to any brother minister who desired his services.

He Lived Under Stress Enough
to "Kill the Strongest of men"

Many of us wondered how he lived under the tremendous strain, occasioned by the amount of preaching he went through, and the nights he spent in prayer, which seemed enough to kill the strongest of men, but on he went like an express train, determined to reach its destination without hindrance; his eyes steadily fixed upon his crucified, buried, risen, ascended, pleading and coming Lord. And all the powers of hell could not move him from his soul's centre.

And now the brave soldier's precious form lies beneath the ocean waves, and his blood-washed spirit is present with the Lord in yon land of light and glory, the homeland of all who love and serve the Christ of God.

Farewell, beloved soldier, we shall meet you in the morning without a cloud.

Chapter 9

God Trusted Him to be the Titanic's Final Witness

Tribute by Mr. John Paton,
of Carmyle

I am thankful to have the opportunity of putting on record how much I owe in my Christian life to friend-ship with dear John Harper. I have found the word of *Proverbs 17:27* ("A man of understanding is of an excellent spirit.") to be true indeed, and the two friends now with the Lord who had most to do with the "sharpening" of my life were Matthew Colquhoun and John Harper.

Burning Zeal

Both were close friends, not only of my own, but of each other, and oftentimes before he fell on sleep on 6th May, 1909, did Matthew serve the Lord at Paisley Road during John Harper's pastorate. The one impressed me tremendously by the sweet and trans-parent holiness of his life, the other no less by his burning and devoted zeal, both qualities being manifestly born of their ardent love to the Saviour. When one

Mr. John Paton

*Some of us can well imagine him
in these last awful minutes
on board the doomed Titanic,
standing amidst a group of stricken,
repentant souls pointing them to the
Saviour he had loved and served so well,
and helping them to seize their
eleventh-hour opportunity.*

experiences how easy it is to allow the keen edge of spiritual life to dull, one prizes the privilege of such friendships as these, and how many of the rank and file of our Christian community, like myself, must have been blessed through contact with these two lives, eternity alone will reveal.

To Spend and be Spent

To be in the company of John Harper was to have created anew in one's heart the desire to "spend and be spent" in the Master's service. Some of us can well imagine him in these last awful minutes on board the doomed *Titanic*, standing amidst a group of stricken, repentant souls pointing them to the Saviour he had loved and served so well, and helping them to seize their eleventh-hour opportunity.

God has not many servants whom He could trust with such a service, and that to me at least is the explanation of our brother being on board the *Titanic* instead of on the *Lusitania* as he had at one time planned.

May we all follow John Harper in so far as he followed Jesus.

Chapter 10

An Overwhelming Vision

Tribute by Mr. Robert Logan,
Evangelist

The sudden and unexpected end of our beloved brother, Mr. Harper, came to those of us who knew him and loved him as a staggering blow, and even yet we feel it difficult to think of him as having departed from the scene of his zealous, self-sacrificing, and fruitful labours.

The Strength of his Personal Life

Mr. Harper was a strong man. He was strong in his love to the brethren. The grip of his kindly hand and his brotherly salutation were always cheering.

He was strong in his love and reverence for the Bible. His progress in Bible study and Bible knowledge was very striking.

He was strong in his love for prayer. He knew as few men seemed to know that true power with men must be preceded with communion with God. Hence with him it was not the ordinary ten or fifteen minutes of waiting upon God. He spent hours in persistent wrestling with God in prayer for the

Mr. Robert Logan, Evangelist

But oh! how he burned,
prayed, laboured and wept
for the conversion of sinners
and, blessed be God,
great numbers were led
to the Saviour's feet
through his consecrated efforts.

salvation of perishing souls. Oh for a mighty increase of such intercessors!

The Strength of his Concern for Others

He was strong in his love for the perishing. He had an intense love for souls. He was eager for the sanctification of saints. But oh! how he burned, prayed, laboured and wept for the conversion of sinners; and, blessed be God, great numbers were led to the Saviour's feet through his consecrated efforts.

The Source of his Strength

He was strong in his love for the Saviour who died for him. He lived, walked, prayed and preached under the sense of an overwhelming vision of Calvary. Hence Christ and Him crucified was ever his theme. To him the name of Jesus was sweet, sacred, and precious. May his mantle fall upon not a few of us so that we may successfully run the race that is set before us, until the day dawns when we shall meet to part no more.

The contents of his (Harper's) letter
were mainly along the lines
of urging to incessant activity
for the ingathering of the lost,
and the up-building of the saints,
and encouraging myself personally
to go on in the work
among the fallen and the outcast.

Chapter 11

A Man of Tender Counsel and Encouragement

Tribute by Mr. Alex. Galbraith, Seamen's Missionary, Glasgow

My acquaintance and fellowship with dear brother John Harper, whom I loved in the Lord, goes back for at least twelve or fourteen years. I saw the man develop and grow spiritually, in zeal for the souls of men, and in loyalty to Christ and His truth.

My last communication from him was about a week before he appeared at the Noon Meeting in March for the last time, and the contents of his letter were mainly along the lines of urging to incessant activity for the ingathering of the lost, and the up-building of the saints, and encouraging myself personally to go on in the work among the fallen and the outcast; and the tenderness of his words of counsel and encouragement are with me still.

Chapter 12

When he Spoke, Souls Cried out for Mercy

Tribute by Pastor M. Ferguson,
Armiesland

It was my privilege and joy to know the late Pastor John Harper for over twelve years. I first heard of him at New Cumnock, where he had been holding some meetings. The church formed there by Mr. James Adair was looking out for a pastor and were very keen to secure Mr. Harper. I saw the fruits of his mission, and felt any church would be justified in securing such a man of God.

I afterwards met him in the Gordon Halls, Paisley Road, and when I saw the spirit and enthusiasm of the meetings, I said to one of the workers, "You won't keep Mr. Harper long here."

Constant Revival

Well, he was not to be so easily lifted out of Paisley Road. He found his sphere there for many years, and hundreds will thank God through all eternity for his faithful ministry in that

Pastor Malcolm Ferguson

*After Mrs. Harper's death
he would often stay over-night in the
church and pray for the occupants of
every seat, and then on Sabbath
he would look for and expect
souls to be saved.
He was a burning and a shining light.*

place. Others will tell the tale of the church, its enlargement, its constant revivals, the overflowing crowds, and the hundreds of souls saved and blessed.

Great Crowds and Great Conviction

I was often there during 1905, when the news of the Welsh Revival spread. I did not go to Wales, but often saw scenes in Paisley Road Church similar to what we heard were going on there. The crowds were so great it was difficult to get in, and after getting in, still more difficult to get near the platform. Then, before any one could speak ten minutes, souls were crying out for mercy under the mighty power of God. It was not excitement. It was the Holy Spirit convicting of sin. One was forced to ask often, What is the secret of this perennial blessing in Paisley Road? But when in touch with the Pastor in his vestry or in his home, the secret was soon found out.

"Closeted With God"

Nobody could be in Mr. Harper's presence long till it was found what a mighty man of God he was, especially in prayer. He knew God. He knew his Bible, and he knew by heart-felt experience the indwelling power of the Holy Spirit. He had a passion-ate love for Christ and souls. It often amazed me the amount of work Mr. Harper went through. When he studied, and how he prepared the marvelous addresses he gave, was a wonder to many. But when most of us were sleeping he was in the secret place of the Most High, closeted with God and His Word all night in the little room off the vestry in Paisley Road Church.

Whole Nights of Prayer

After Mrs. Harper's death he would often stay over-night in the church and pray for the occupants of every seat, and then on Sabbath he would look for and expect souls to be saved. He was a burning and a shining light. Some burn and don't shine; others shine but don't burn. When he spoke it might be said what was said by the man who went to hear Rowland Hill, "The words come hissing hot from his heart." He believed what he preached, and preached what he believed. Christ and eternal things were all so real to him. He lived and preached "as if Christ died yesterday, arose to-day, and was coming tomorrow."

He Sensed the Presence of God

If ever a preacher was conscious of the presence of God it was Mr. Harper. I once heard him say at a conference, "We won't get many sinners convicted and converted through laughs and jokes. Some have laughed the Spirit of God out of Gospel meetings, and the one thing we are conscious of above all others in many meetings, is the lack of the deep sense of the presence and power of God."

"You Will be Missed"

We say of him what Jonathan said of David: "You will be missed for your place will be vacant." How some of us miss him! his cheery word, his helpful messages, and above all the inspiration of his magnetic presence. I never left his company but I came home to pray. This was invariably the effect Mr. Harper's presence had on me.

May a double portion of his holy, consecrated spirit fall on those of us who are left a little while longer, not only to "Hold the fort," but to storm the forts of darkness as our brother loved to do.

Chapter 13

John Harper's Parting Text

Tribute by
Pastor Wm. Wright

Denny and surrounding district are much indebted to God for the gift of Mr. John Harper. I felt there was a manifestation of Christ in his life that I had not known before. We had on one occasion a conversation about the indwelling of Christ, and he suggested our need of being "strengthened with might by His Spirit in the inner man," that Christ might dwell in our hearts by faith. Early in life he had experienced this strengthening process, and when he came to Denny it was seen in a marvelous degree.

He believed in having the text he was to preach from direct from God, and I have seen his soul in great trouble until he had the witness of the Holy Spirit in regard to the passage of Scripture he was to expound. He also had the stamp of heaven on the title he gave to the subjects he preached about, and his divisions were masterly.

My parting with him
near the station at Old Cumnock,
last March,
was an incident worth remembering.
We agreed to give each other a text . . .
The text he gave me
was one that had been much in his mind
for a considerable time,
"He that doeth the will of God
abideth for ever" (I John 2:17).

Denny, Scotland is Shaken for God

Denny is not easily moved, but when he had the town placarded with bills asking, "Is there a hell?" It made some stop and think. He announced one subject that has remained with me: "The hardest thing in the world," which he proved to be to go to hell, from *2nd Peter 3 and 9*, as the sinner has to go there against the will of God.

Green Fields and White Fields

In September, 1910, he delivered one of the freshest and most hopeful messages I have ever heard. The subject was "Green fields and white fields." The fields were green in the eyes of the disciples, they were white to the harvest in the eyes of our Lord. In delivering a mighty message from God during the same short mission, he raised a question for the evolutionists to answer, in this form: "If the status of human character is continually rising, how is it that the One Who is almost universally recognized as the perfect man, Jesus, existed nearly nineteen hundred years ago?"

Fighting the Forces of Hell

It was Harper's firm conviction that Satan would have killed him if he could. He was continually conscious, especially in the latter years of his ministry, of the conflict going on in every service between the powers of light and the powers of darkness. He gave me a little hint personally last September in London that has been very helpful to my soul to this effect: "The devil cannot touch you on resurrection ground." Although often assailed by Satan, he enjoyed in a superlative degree the rest of God.

Nine years ago I asked him the question, "In the Gospel what takes the place of the fourth commandment?" His instant reply was, "The rest of God."

To the uninitiated his removing from Glasgow to London looked like a wrong step, but a revived church in London, and other churches influenced for good, proved it to be the mind of the Spirit which he had followed in leaving Paisley Road for Walworth Road.

Parting Words From John Harper

My parting with him near the station at Old Cumnock, last March, was an incident worth remembering. We agreed to give each other a text. I gave him the one, "Feed my lambs," which led him to make this noteworthy statement: When he was in Chicago he was earnestly engaged in secret prayer, when God, by His Holy Spirit, gave the assurance to him that his little daughter, six years of age, was a Christian. I thanked God and him most sincerely for the beautiful story, and all the more because I am convinced that this is where many are up against the will of God today, in not recognizing believing children as the lambs of the flock.

The text he gave me was one that had been much in his mind for a considerable time, "He that doeth the will of God abideth for ever" *(I John 2:17).*

Chapter 14

His Strength Came out of Weakness

Tribute by
Mr. Wm. R. Andrew of Glasgow

It is hard to realize that the friend and brother who was so much to us has been removed from this scene of labour, and that we shall never again here join heart and hand with him in proclaiming the love of Jesus to this poor sin-stricken world.

Yet it *is* true. He has gone to higher service, called up higher by his Lord, whom he so truly loved and followed. What joy must be our dear brother's now as he gazes upon the face of Jesus—upon the One who even here had ravished his heart with His love.

I first met Mr. Harper nearly fourteen years ago, shortly after the commencement of his ministry in the Gordon Halls, Paisley Road. Since then it was my privilege and joy to be with him from time to time, sometimes in Paisley Road Church, and sometimes in other parts of Scotland, labouring in the service of the Master. After each of these seasons of fellowship, whether short or more protracted, the impression received at the first meeting was deepened and strengthened. Here was a man who knew God, and one who knew how to reach God in prayer!

Mr. William R. Andrew

*In private life in Chicago
Mr. Harper was bright and joyful,
and though at times
he was ill and suffered great pain,
which was aggravated by over-work,
he gloried in his weakness,
because thereby the power of Christ
was manifested in him.*

After Mr. Harper left Glasgow for London it was my great delight to join him on several occasions in the work of publishing in that great city and in Wales, the old Gospel story of Jesus and His Love.

When he requested me by cable to proceed to Chicago, an immediate departure was arranged, and I reached him in the first week in December last. The fight had been strenuous, and though it had been followed by sweeping victory, our brother was tired and not over-well. He expressed satisfaction at the "*sight* of a weel-kent face frae Bonnie Scotland," and he seemed comforted. He was doing his work in his usual style—morning prayer meeting at six o'clock, another prayer meeting at noon, Bible reading in the afternoon, and public meeting in the evening. The gaps between the meetings were filled up with interviews, visits, funerals, and attempts to meet the other innumerable demands that were made upon his time.

The Holy Spirit was
Discernibly at Work in Him

Throughout the entire visit the fact that God's Holy Spirit was undoubtedly at work was easily discernible. Deep conviction of sin, confession, restitution on the part of many, conflict with those of God's people who were compromising with the world, warfare with principalities and powers and spiritual hosts of darkness—these were the evidences in these meetings of His working.

The preaching of our brother was in demonstration of the Spirit and of power. His themes were the Cross of Christ, God's marvelous grace to man, and the soon coming of our Lord Jesus Christ. His messages on grace held his audiences spell-bound by the hour. As the Spirit of God carried the truth home to the hearts of his hearers, he called upon them to yield, repeating over and over again the words of a favorite chorus:

> "Nay, but I yield, I yield,
>   I can hold out no more.
> I sink, by dying love constrained,
>   and own Thee conqueror."

The message of *Galatians* 2:20, "I am crucified with Christ: nevertheless I live: yet not I, but Christ liveth in me: and the life which I now live in the flesh I live by the faith of the Son of God, who loved me, and gave himself for me," was another upon which our dear brother laid great emphasis. Often he would have the audience repeat the words of that text carefully and prayerfully, and, as they did so, many entered into a new conception of its meaning, and a new experience of its truth by accepting "God's reckoning alone."

The Song on John Harper's Lips

The following words of a hymn were many times upon his own lips:

> "Buried with Christ and raised with Him too,
>   What is there left for me to do?
> Simply to cease from struggle and strife,
>   Simply to walk in newness of life."

In private life in Chicago Mr. Harper was bright and joyful, and though at times he was ill and suffered great pain, which was aggravated by over-work, he gloried in his weakness, because thereby the power of Christ was manifested in him.

A Sympathetic Listener

In any spare time he had he was at the disposal of those who came, as many did each day, some to confess sin, and to be helped, guided, and prayed with. He was a loving, sympathetic listener to many tales of sorrow and wrongdoing, and nothing was a trouble to him, and nothing a sacrifice if by any means he might save some.

His preparation for all this service was in his prayer-life. What was witnessed and shared of that was a never-to-be-forgotten privilege. Often after a hard day's work he would reach his room tired out and much in need of rest and sleep, but something else claimed him. Instead of retiring he threw himself on his knees at the bedside, and by the hour he poured out his soul in agonizing prayer to God that salvation and blessing might come to those in Chicago, and London, and Scotland, who were refusing the message of the Spirit. Friends were mentioned by name–those with whom he had been associated in Gospel work during the years of his ministry, and many as well about whose salvation he was concerned.

A Voice With "Tones" of Love

There was a touch of softness and love and intimacy in the very tones of his voice as, in prayer, he used the beloved name, "Lord Jesus." It was evident that even then our brother had gone far into the presence of his Lord. Then ceasing prayer for a time, he would turn to the Word. The teaching that fell from his lips was wonderful as he gave expression to some new unfolding of truth which the "Lord Jesus" had just given him. The Lord, the Spirit, spoke through him indeed.

John Harper has "gone before" us to the larger service. May his God and ours make us faithful as he was while we still labour here.

"Greater love hath no man than this, that a man lay down his life for his friends" *(John 15:13)*.

We owe all we are, humanly speaking,
to the inspiration that came
from his consecrated life,
and our only desire is to follow on
to know the Lord, walking humbly
and prayerfully before our God,
so that He may be honoured
and glorified by our daily lives.

Chapter 15

"John Harper Led my Wife and me to Christ"

Testimony I

Saturday, 9th August, 1902, was a day of great rejoicing on earth, because on that day our late King Edward was coronated amidst pomp and pageantry, and London was the centre of hundreds of representatives of other nations who were present at the magnificent event. The day following, Sabbath, 10th August, 1902, was a day of great rejoicing to me, because on that day my wife and I coronated Jesus Christ, and owned him King of our lives.

Work had been going on for about a year before this in the little "tin kirk," as the corrugated iron church, was called (in which were held the services of the Paisley Road Baptist Church, under the ministry of Pastor John Harper). The services were well attended, and very aggressive work was being carried on in the open-air just before our conversion. We had never been in a Baptist Church in our lives, but had seen Mr. Harper in the centre of his workers at the open-air meeting, at the corner of Plantation Street and Paisley Road, several times as we went up the street to Paisley Road.

On Friday night, 7th August, 1902 two workers from the Baptist Church knocked at the door of my wife's mother's house (we were not married then) and invited her to the Gospel Meeting in the iron church on Sabbath night, at 6.30. When I went to see her on the Saturday night she told me of the visit, and asked me if I would care to go with her. I usually attended another church, and did not much care about leaving our own church for a night even, and going to another.

However, I consented, and the next night found me for the first time inside a Baptist Church. It was crowded. We received a hearty handshake from two deacons at the door, and a hymn book was put into our hands. The singing was hearty, with no stiffness about it. But the sermon—well, I don't know what the preacher said, but I remember his text: "He feedeth on ashes" *(Isaiah 44:20)*.

"Every Word cut, and I Felt Convicted of my Sins"

Pastor Harper was the preacher, and oh! how he did preach. Every word cut, and I felt convicted of sin, and knew there and then that I needed salvation. Not a word do I remember of the sermon, but the earnestness and burning passion of the preacher arrested me. I had never heard preaching like it, so powerful and so pleading, that when the sermon was over and a young man and young woman got up and sang the sweet duet, "Covered by the Blood of Jesus," I drank in the words of the hymn as a thirsty traveler under a burning sun drinks the clear sparkling water from the spring at the wayside. Little did I know that I was beginning to drink of that Living Water from the Eternal Spring, which, if a man drink of, he will never thirst again.

The duet was finished, and a time of prayer followed. Then Mr. Harper asked for all those who wanted to trust Jesus Christ as their own personal Saviour to raise their hand, and mine went up. I knew I was a sinner. I knew I needed Christ. I knew enough of the Bible to be aware of the fact that I required to be converted before I could enter the Kingdom of Heaven. That memorable 10th August found me stricken in soul before God, and ripe for salvation. After my hand was raised I settled the question of my soul's salvation by accepting Jesus Christ as my Saviour.

No one spoke to me. No one prayed with me. No one read texts to me. The transaction took place between my Lord and me, and it was blessedly real. I knew that Sabbath night, sitting on the third back seat of the church, at the preacher's right hand, that my sins were forgiven, and I was born of God. Jesus can speak the word of peace to a soul.

"My Wife Nearly Took a fit"

In the after meeting a dear brother who is now in glory came up to my wife and asked her if she was trusting Jesus. She said, "No." Then he spoke to her the Words of Life, but still she could not see the truth of salvation. He left speaking to her for a moment and turned to me and asked if I was saved. I said, "Yes," and my wife nearly took a fit. "That's not true," she said. She thought I had just said so to get rid of the man. She could not under-stand how I could be saved seeing no one spoke to me, nor read the Bible to me. But the Spirit of God had spoken to me. The Christian brother asked me how long was it since I trusted Christ, and I said, "When I raised my hand at the first meeting." He then turned again to my wife, told her of his conversion, and while telling her this, the light broke in, and she too was saved.

Praise God, for His wondrous love and grace. Both saved the same night. That is over nine years ago, and from that to this we have gone on our way, "Kept by the power of God, through faith, unto salvation." Three months afterwards we were baptized on our confession of faith in the Lord Jesus Christ, by Pastor Harper, and received into fellowship, and have continued in fellowship with the Church at Paisley Road since then.

We owe all we are to his Inspiration

We have often thanked God that He led us to Paisley Road Baptist Church that night, 10th August, 1902, and that he privileged us to have ever known Mr. Harper. How he watched over us, praying for us, feeding us "on the finest of the wheat and honey from the rock," and carefully and wisely counseling us. We owe all we are, humanly speaking, to the inspiration that came from his consecrated life, and our only desire is to follow on to know the Lord, walking humbly and prayerfully before our God, so that He may be honoured and glorified by our daily lives.

Our hearts were stricken when we heard of his tragic end, and yet me thinks he would rather have been taken away suddenly than lie on a bed with a lingering illness. He has now entered into his rest, and his works do follow him. But the memory of his life will be an inspiration to all that knew him, and his burning zeal, yearning passion, loyal devotion, and intense earnestness cannot but have left their stamp upon those who sat under his ministry.

Farewell, dear pastor, and father in the Gospel, may your children seek to walk worthy of the vocation unto which they are called. May the truths you have so often preached bear fruit in their lives. May your example of holy abandonment to the Will of God emulate others to follow, even as you followed, Christ. And may your eyes even now rest on us all seeking to do the Will of God, and going on unto perfection. And yet it is not "Farewell," but only "Good-night." A few more days and then we'll all meet to part no more in that land of song and joy, where there are no more partings, and no more tears, no more pain, and no more sorrow, no more death, and no more sin. Thank God, no more sin,

> "Until the day dawns
>   and the shadows flee away."
> "Sleep on beloved, sleep and take thy rest,
>   Lay down thy head upon thy Saviour's breast,

We loved thee well–but Jesus loves thee best,
    Goodnight. Good-night. Good-night."

"They that be wise shall shine as the brightness of the firmament, and they that turn many to righteousness, as the stars for ever and ever" *(Daniel 12:3)*.

P. C. M.

*For the first time in my life
I was dealt with about my soul, and that
night I was brought to a
knowledge of the truth.*

Chapter 16

A Drunkard Found Deliverance

Testimony II

As a brand plucked from the burning I am thankful to God for His long-suffering and mercy, in that He did not cut me off in my sins. I had gone about as far as a man could go in the pleasures and follies of sin in drinking and gambling, and had on several occasions broken up my home and well-nigh ruined my business. It was while I was thus running on in my wild career that I was apprehended by the grace of God.

On Saturday night, 6th November, 1897 I was as drunk as I could be, and on the Sunday night following was reaping what I had sowed. To while away the time I took a walk along Paisley Road with a friend who introduced me to two of the church members of the Baptist Church which had been formed about two months before, with Mr. Harper as pastor.

For the first time in my life I was dealt with about my soul, and that night I was brought to a knowledge of the truth, being enabled from the heart to say, "I will trust, and not be afraid." Since then I have been a wonder unto many. God Himself wrought the change. That night my wife was also enabled to close in with offered mercy, and since then we have journeyed to Zion together. Instead of strong drink being followed after, I am satisfied with the living water which springs up into everlasting life.

Instead of gambling and worrying about what I might win I have, by the grace of God, found the winner in Jesus Christ. Instead of blaspheming and using profane language I have a new song in my mouth.

God has kept me by His grace for fourteen and a half years. To Him be all the glory. I am saved by grace through faith in Jesus who finished the work of my redemption on the Cross. There is one Mediator between God and Men, the Man Christ Jesus, and I believe in Him. Praise His Holy Name.

J.B.

All I am I owe, under God,
to our late dearly beloved
and much lamented
Pastor John Harper,
who was to me a father and brother,
watching over me, praying for me,
and instructing me
in the new life.

Chapter 17

"John Harper was, To me, a Father"

Testimony III

My heart's desire and prayer to God is that some man who, like myself, has had the bitter and humiliating experience of innumerable trials and failures to lift himself out of sin, may on reading this humble testimony, trust Jesus Christ the only Saviour, and join with me in His praises.

I was a Roman Catholic by birth, education, training and profession, learned to drink, and to indulge in many other sins as well. While still very young I joined the army where the drink passion grew stronger, and led a very loose life. I served my time; returned home with the drink habit stronger than ever. Both in the service and in civil life.

I made several attempts to break away from drunkenness and other sins by going to confession, taking pledges, making resolutions, etc., but all to no avail. I could not save myself, and I often thought, "What is the good of all these confessions, etc., when, each time I am as bad and often worse than before?" until one Saturday night, the 14th January, 1905, I found myself in the Iron Church, Plantation Street, again under the influence of drink. It was a time of revival, and every one seemed so intensely happy. The service went on, but I can't tell much about what was taking place, only that I got very unhappy and convinced that I was a very great sinner, and had been leading a very bad life.

Thank God, a Christian man took notice of me and came over and sat down beside me. He was the means in God's hand of leading me to the Saviour. But it was not without a painful struggle. Satan brought up every possible and impossible reason why I should not trust Christ as my Saviour. But when I trusted Him the joy and peace and sense of a new power more than made up for all.

Without the slightest doubt or fear I felt and knew that I was saved, and, thank God, I know it now. "I am not all I ought to be, but I am not what I used to be." All I am I owe, under God, to our late dearly beloved and much lamented Pastor John Harper, who was to me a father and brother, watching over me, praying for me, and instructing me in the new life.

Four days after my conversion, my wife was led to the Saviour. Three months later we were baptized, and joined the Church. I am now one of the deacons, having been appointed to the office a few months ago.

H. P.

I owe very much
to my dear late Pastor Mr. Harper,
for his teaching and inspiration,
and for the encouragement he gave me
to be out and out for God.
I praise God for the privilege
of sitting under him for 12 years,
and for being engaged
in the Lord's work with him
during that time.

Chapter 18

A Helpless Prodigal's Debt to John Harper

Testimony IV

I was a poor helpless sinner, held by the power of strong drink and a blaspheming tongue. I tried to repent by going to Church and taking the pledge, but it proved of no avail. A special mission was being held in the Baptist Church, in Gordon Halls. I had a brother a member of the Church. Special prayer was made for me. God heard and answered prayer. By invitation I went to one of the services. At the close one of the deacons spoke to me and asked if I was saved, or would I like to be. He read to me *John 3:16*, and showed me that "whosoever" meant anyone and must mean me. I trusted Christ that night, 11th October, 1898.

Mr. Harper came to the house next morning to see if I had confessed Christ, which I had done, and have done ever since. I am what I am by the grace of God. I owe very much to my dear late Pastor Mr. Harper, for his teaching and inspiration, and for the encouragement he gave me to be out and out for God. I praise God for the privilege of sitting under him for 12 years, and for being engaged in the Lord's work with him during that time. I now hold the position of a deacon, I, who was once a poor drunkard and blasphemer. But I found mercy through the Lord Jesus Christ.

"To God be all the glory, great things he hath done."

A. M. L.

Oh! what grace
that trans-forms a poor drunkard,
a seller of whisky,
and a deep-dyed sinner,
such as I was,
into a son of God
and a child of His love.
All I owe in my spiritual life
I owe to the influence and teaching
of Mr. Harper,
who taught me the things of God,
and whose life was
an inspiration to me.

Chapter 19

A "Deep-dyed" Sinner is Cleansed

Testimony V

Thank God for His saving grace in lifting a poor sinner like me from the dunghill, and setting me among princes. I was brought up a Presbyterian, but had no knowledge of God's salvation. As a lad, when living in Greenock, I went into the spirit trade with the determination to avoid the drink in any form, and not to taste it. But I soon fell under its power and dominion, and became a confirmed drunkard. I got so used to it that I could drink all the day long, and yet one could hardly tell it on me.

I was 12 years selling the cursed stuff behind a public-house counter, and all these years I did not go home a single night sober. I left the drink trade and went to a lemonade manufacturer. But that was as bad, as I supplied the public-houses with aerated waters, and got drunk there as well.

At the age of 25 I came to Glasgow and went into the employment of P. & W. M'Lellan, at Clutha Iron Works. But still I was a victim to strong drink. I was gripped by the giant evil, and could not get free of its power.

One night, at New Year, 1901, I took very ill, and the doctor was sent for. He said I had only three hours to live. This then was the end of my drinking; three hours – and then hell. I knew that was where I was going to. I knew there was no hope, but yet I prayed that God would spare me, and I would stop drinking, and live a better life. He did spare me, and for two years after I struggled against my love for whisky and beer, but still drank wine.

Harper Awakened me to my Need for Christ

I determined to pay a visit to every church in Glasgow, to see if I could hear of something that would bring me rest and peace. One Sunday evening, 1st November, 1903, I found myself in the Baptist Church, in Plantation Street, and heard Mr. Harper preach. A young lady sang "Over the dead line," and I felt that if I did not accept Jesus Christ I would pass over that dead line and be lost.

No one spoke to me. I was so awakened to my need of Christ, that I knew all I had to do was accept Him as my Savour. I did so, and now after eight and a half years of victory over drink and sin I can say that God's Word is true, "If any man be in Christ he is a new creature, old things are passed away; behold, all things are become new." *(2 Cor. 5:17).*

A new World

I was in a new world. The drink desire was gone. Peace filled my soul. I knew from the moment I said, "Lord, I'll trust Thee, sink or swim, I'll trust Thee," that I was saved, and, thank God, I have been kept ever since by His mighty power and grace. About a year after, I was baptized, and joined the Church.

The Impact of Mr. Harper's Life

I am now a deacon in the Church. Oh! what grace that trans-forms a poor drunkard, a seller of whisky, and a deep-dyed sinner, such as I was, into a son of God and a child of His love. All I owe in my spiritual life I owe to the influence and teaching of Mr. Harper, who taught me the things of God, and whose life was an inspiration to me.

May God help some poor drunkard to trust in my Saviour, and find that "Wherefore he is able also to save them to the uttermost that come unto God by him, seeing he ever liveth to make intercession for them." *(Hebrews 7:25).*

J. C.

What we are in the Christian life
we owe to our late lamented pastor,
Mr. Harper, whose godly life
and holy example proved such a help to us,
and who looked after us
as carefully as a father
after his children,
and brought us to love
the study of Scripture and
the joy of waiting upon God in prayer.

Chapter 20

Harper Overcame Arms of Rebellion
Testimony VI

I just want to give my humble testimony to the saving and keeping power of the Lord Jesus Christ, who has 15 years. It was on the 27th October, 1897, mother was giving a Halloween party, and I was asked to bring up my sweetheart for her tea. Little did I think that it was for the purpose of getting me into touch with Mr. Harper that the party had been arranged. At length the night came, and we were all gathered in the room, and to my great surprise who did I see in the room but Mr. Harper and several members of the Church (one of them now the senior deacon of the Church).

My mother was a member of the Church, being amongst the first number that was at the start of the Church in the Gordon Halls. Of course, I knew what would happen after tea–I would be spoken to about my soul. Well, we had our tea, and then after a little conversation I thought it was time for me to get out. It was getting too warm for me, so I got up to get my cap, but could not find it. It had been removed from its place.

But I went out with my bare head, but I did not stop long as it was a cold night, so I had to go back to the house again, for the purpose of getting some covering for my head. Little did I think I was to get a covering for my sins.

"I Threw Down my Arms of Rebellion"

When I got to the house, an elderly brother got hold of me and spoke to me about Christ. In the corner of the room Mr. Harper was dealing with my sweetheart about her soul. Shortly after, Mr. Harper engaged in prayer thanking God for her decision. I then threw down the arms of rebellion and accepted Christ also as my Saviour and Lord. The Scriptures we saw the light through, were *Isaiah 53:6*, "All we like sheep," etc., and *Romans 10:9*, "If thou shalt confess with thy mouth the Lord Jesus, and shalt believe in thine heart that God hath raised him from the dead, thou shalt be saved."

That eventful night will never be erased from our memories, and we were baptized shortly afterwards, and joined the Church. After over 14 years experience of Christ's love and salvation we can say that His grace is sufficient for us, and His strength is made perfect in weakness.

"Mr. Harper Looked After us as Carefully as a Father After his Children"

What we are in the Christian life we owe to our late lamented pastor, Mr. Harper, whose godly life and holy example proved such a help to us, and who looked after us as carefully as a father after his children, and brought us to love the study of Scripture and joy of waiting upon God in prayer.

Would to God I could pray like him, and now that he is in the presence of the Lord whom he so much loved and so loyally served, our only desire is to follow in his steps even as he followed Christ.

C. B. and Mrs. B.

As Mr. Harper went on,
my conviction deepened,
and I saw I needed a Saviour.
There I surrendered my all,
and I have been going on my way
rejoicing ever since.

Chapter 21

Harper's Words Brought Deep Conviction

Testimony VII

On the Sabbath evening of July 4, 1897, I went to hear Mr. Harper. The text he spoke from was Revelation 3:20, "Behold, I stand at the door and knock." I had been convicted for some time, and, as Mr. Harper went on, my conviction deepened, and I saw I needed a Saviour.

There I surrendered my all, and I have been going on my way rejoicing ever since. It has not always been sunshine, but Christ is all in all to me. I am a member of Paisley Road Baptist Church, and so is my wife.

S. M. K.

*I was convicted of sin
saw my need of a Saviour,
and there and then
surrendered to Christ.*

John Harper

A very little while and He will come,
and the door will be shut,
and the door of Christendom sealed.
Only a brief season can remain for us all.
But what may not be done
in these quickly passing days!

Chapter 22

A Message From John Harper

Delivered in 1911 at the
Moody Church in Chicago

Vision, compassion, intercession–these are three great
links in the golden chain of redemptive service. How clearly
you can see them in the saving ministry and life service of our
Lord Jesus Himself. He saw the multitudes as sheep without a
shepherd–scattered, torn, bruised, and bleeding–and if that
was the vision before His eyes when He looked on a multitude
from the quiet religious villages of Galilee, where the people
were moral in their habits of life, and not sunken with drink
and manifold vice, what would be the vision before Him if He
looked to-day on Chicago?

"Pray ye"

With that vision His heart was moved with com-passion,
agitated with deep feeling–agonized within Him, would be a
better word. He had compassion on them, taking their pain
and sorrow up into His own heart of love, and with that
love-swept spirit He turns to His disciples and says, "Pray
ye," and on every possible occasion slips off Himself to the

lonely mountain side to spend the night or early morning hours in prayer.

Give us "men of the Mountain Solitude and Midnight Watch"

Beloved, how few of us have the Master's vision, and hence, how few of us have the compassion-filled heart, the consequent ministry of intercession! If any one conviction has laid hold of my spirit more than another, and has held it in a grasp as solemn as eternity for some years past, it is that the overwhelming need of the church and the doomed world is intercessors—not so much preachers, however great that need is—but men of the mountain solitude and midnight watch, who know how to stand between God and men, in fasting and prayer; and who will not leave the throne of grace until from His presence will go forth times of refreshing and salvation that will make His name a praise in the earth.

Then will be given to the church, preachers with the tongues of fire, and workers mantled with His power; and the whole awakened Spirit-filled church will become the instrument of our glorified Lord in awakening a god-less world to the conviction of sin and sense of need of the atoning blood, and to the fear of coming wrath.

"The Door Will be Shut"

A very little while and He will come, and the door will be shut, and the door of Christendom sealed. Only a brief season can remain for us all. But what may not be done in these quickly passing days! What seasons of prayer and intercession may we not have! What sacrifices for Him may we not make! What power from the throne may we not receive! What scenes of blessing may we not witness in the gathering out of the last members of the body of Christ from this doomed and darkening world, while upon it the night shadows of coming judgment are falling fast!

Beyond this little while there will be the glory of His presence, the glad reunion with the loved, the thrilling "well done" of the Master at His judgment seat–the entering in, to go out no more forever.

But there will be no more opportunity of praying lost souls to His feet and winning them to His heart forever.

See, faithful to Christ, his Master,
Intent on the task He gave,
On the eve of the dire disaster
One is telling His power to save.

Chapter 23

Beautiful in the Morning

The night before the *Titanic* sank Mr. Harper was seen earnestly seeking to lead a young man to Christ. Afterwards, when on deck, seeing a glint of red in the west, he said, "It will be beautiful in the morning."

Oh, fair must it be in the morning,
  When the sunset enkindles the west,
And the clouds, in their golden adorning,
  Creep quietly down to their rest!
Rest we, like them, in the hope that a dawn
  Calm and resplendent comes marching on.

Ah, drear is the tale of the morning,
  And awesome the wail in the tide,
When the hand of the Ice-King, unwarning,
  Tears open the vessel's side,
And into the depths of the ruthless deep
  Thrusts multitudes fast in their final sleep.

Yet fair must it be in the morning,
  If fair did the sun go down.

God's heroes, the death-trammels spurning,
    Press up to the victor's crown.
Where then is thy victory, vaunting grave,
    When ours is the SAVIOUR, Mighty to save?

See, faithful to Christ, his Master,
    Intent on the task He gave,
On the eve of the dire disaster
    One is telling His power to save.
If sinks the sun with so pure a light,
    It will rise again both serene and bright.

The death of the righteous who dieth
    Is gateway to life evermore;
The joy that all glories outvieth
    For him is laid up in store.
Painless and tearless,
    with "no more sea,"
Beauteous indeed
    shall the morning be.

Horace E. Govan

Chapter 24

A Pattern For Christian Workers

A Sermon Outline by John Harper

"Stephen, a man full of faith and the Holy Ghost"
(Acts vi. 5)

How comforting and. inspiring it is to note that Stephen was filled with the Holy Ghost as a *man*, not as a minister; and how searching it is to remember that his appointment to office in the Church depended on that fullness. Let us note that these words suggest :

I. A DOUBLE FULNESS OF BLESSING.

1. FULL OF FAITH,

Certainly he never would have been full of the Holy Ghost, if not first full of faith and on the other hand, full of faith because filled with the spirit of faith. What does this fullness mean?

(a) To be filled with confidence in God; all doubt and uncertainty gone; and to be fully assured of God's faithfulness, and His willingness, and His sufficiency. And with such assurance must come the very calm and peace of God into the heart.

(b) To be filled with *capacity* for God. Faith makes room for God, and to be full of faith is to have capacity for God in every part of your being; and there is never capacity for God that He does not fill up perfectly, What a wealth of possibility is suggested by that little phrase—" full of faith."

2. FULL OF THE HOLY GHOST,'

Very reverently let it be, said such a fullness defies description and final analysis. But a few thoughts may help to a clearer apprehension of its meaning.

(a) It means to be *full of God*. The Holy Spirit is as truly God as either Jesus or the Father—the passages that prove this are as numerous as those that prove the deity of Jesus—and it is through Him we realize the indwelling of Christ and the presence of the Father. Try to think of what God is, and then think what it must mean to be filled with him.

(b) It means to be *full of Grace*. No grace but is begotten in the heart by the Spirit. Even every thought of holiness is His alone *(see Gal. v. 22)*.

(c) It means to be *full of Glory*. Like the tabernacle or temple of old, filled with the glory of God. The believer, in spirit, soul, and body, is like the tabernacle in construction, with its holy of holies, and holy place, and outer court. And as the glory of God filled the inmost shrine, it flashed out from within; and so, as the Holy Spirit fills the believer's inner being, the glory is manifested through his mortal body. Now the Spirit-filled man has the glory in him, but by-and-bye he will be in the glory, when Christ comes again.

II. A DOUBLE FITNESS FOR SERVICE.

Any man who is not filled with faith can never be fully fitted for the service of the Lord. Doubts fit us for Christ's hospital, but not for his work and warfare. The fullness of faith fits for service because it gives consciousness of the presence of the Lord.

Moses endured as seeing Him who is invisible, and it was faith that gave that vision. It is faith that realizes all the resources of heaven, and gives strength as nothing else can. Finally faith sees the ultimate victory; and without seeing that, no one can serve successfully nor war victoriously. And just as faith gives fitness, so does the fullness of the Spirit. The study of the whole Old and New Testaments on the doctrine of the Spirit will reveal that no man was ever fully conditioned for service without being filled with the Spirit.

In view of the boundless possibilities of a life enjoying this double fullness of blessing and double fitness for service, will not every child of God seek to be Stephen-like, and be thus filled to the glory of God?

Chapter 25

"Christ's Chosen Ones"

A Sermon Outline by John Harper

"They are not of the world, even as I am not of the world"
(John xvii. 16)

1. His chosen ones were given to Him by the Father
    verse 6
2. For them He prays–not for the world
    verse 9
3. They are hated by the world
    verse 14
4. He seeks that they be kept from the evil of the world
    verse 15
5. He sends them as He was sent Himself into the world
    verse 18
6. He desires their unity to convince the worl
    verse 21
7. He shows that the Father is not known to the world
    verse 25

The words of the text (*verse 16*) present to us:

I. A DISTINGUISHING TRUTH
OF THE CHRISTIAN FAITH.

1. Christians are not of the world in the origin of their life—They are born from above.

2. Not of the world in the character of their service—The Christian life consists in doing the will of God.

3. Not of the world in the nature of their conduct—They follow after holiness. They abhor sin.

4. Not of the world in the sources of their joy—Their joy is in God, the world finds pleasure in sin.

5. Not of the world in the theme of their conversation—Their desire is, Tell me more about Jesus.

The words of the text present us:

II. WITH A SEARCHING TEST
FOR THE CHRISTIAN HEART

If not of the world this will be seen—
1. In the hour of bereavement and loss.
2. Amid trial and perplexity.
3. In the decisions and choice we make.
4. In times of prosperity and success.

The words of the text suggest to us:

III. THAT THERE WILL SURELY BE
TRIAL IN THE CHRISTIAN LIFE.

1. The world will reject us.
2. The world will not love us.

Chapter 26

"Who is the Fool?"

A Sermon Outline by John Harper

"*I* have sinned . . . I have played the fool"
(*I Sam. xxvi. 21*)

The text clearly indicates that:

I. THE MAN IS A FOOL WHO SACRIFICES HIS LIFE AT THE SHRINE OF SINFUL INDULGENCE.

"Fools make a mock at sin" (*Proverbs xiv.9*). Another reading is, "Sin makes a mock at fools."

It mocks men by promising what it never performs. Men sacrifice all and gain nothing.

    1. Sin robs of peace of conscience.
    2. Sin robs of purity of mind.
    3. Sin robs of health of body.
    4. Sin robs of the hope of heaven.

II. THE MAN IS A FOOL WHO
SHROUDS HIMSELF IN INFIDELITY.

"The fool hath said in his heart there is no God" *(Psalm xiv.1).*

    1. Is he not a fool who gives up light for darkness?

    2. Is he not a fool who gives up hope for hopelessness?

    3. Is he not a fool who gives up Gospel comfort for a cheerless philosophy?

III. THE MAN IS A FOOL WHO PUTS OFF
DECISION FOR CHRIST TILL HE IS DYING.

He is a fool because he is a *present loser*.

    1. He loses true joy of heart.

    2. He loses peace of conscience.

    3. He loses victory over sin.

    4. He loses capacity to enjoy life.

He may be *an eternal loser*. He may delay till too late.

Chapter 27

"Love to be Remembered"

A Sermon Outline by John Harper

"Draw me, we will run after Thee: the King hath brought me into His chambers; we will be glad and rejoice in Thee, we will remember Thy love more than wine" (Song of *Solomon* *1:4).*

In this verse we have love's three-fold resolve—

I. A RESOLVE TO FOLLOW.

1. It is eager following, "We will run after Thee."
2. It is close following. Not Peter-like, afar off. But David-like, "My soul followeth hard after Thee." Note that it is following, not running *before* Him. "He will run *after thee.*"

II. A RESOLVE TO BE GLAD AND REJOICE.

1. Note the source of the believer's joy. It is "in Thee."
2. Not in the "good ointments" (verse 3)–symbols of the graces He bestows.
3. Not in the "chambers" (verse 4). symbols of the privileges and happy experiences He gives.

4. But "in Thee." All our joy, both passive and active, must be in Him.

III. A RESOLVE TO REMEMBER.

What a memory! We will remember every occasion that He has made us feel the beating of His heart of love to us.

1. We will remember the *fact* of His love. Dare we ever forget this fact?

2. We will remember the *extent* of His love. It reaches down to us in our sin.

3. We will remember the eternity of His love. We cannot go back to its beginnings. We cannot reach to its end. It is eternal. When in His love we are in a circle.

4. We will remember the *purpose* of His love. He loved us that He might save us from our sins, and save us unto Himself.

Note some of the RESULTS THAT FOLLOW from remembering His love:

1. It provides for us a heavenly feast. We obtain a cordial better than wine.

2. It gives us an antidote from fear Joseph Irons puts it thus:

"Thyself I crave,
　　Thy presence is my life, my joy, my heaven,
　　And all without Thyself is dead to me."

Chapter 28

So Great Salvation

"How shall we escape if we neglect so great salvation"
(Hebrew 2:3)

Salvation is God's greatest work. The salvation of a lost world is greater than the creation of a new world. Salvation is great when we consider—

I. THE GREATNESS OF THE PERIL
FROM WHICH IT DELIVERS.

Souls are in danger of being lost.

II. THE GREATNESS OF THE PRICE
PAID TO PROVIDE IT.

The precious blood of Christ is of unspeakable worth.

III. THE GREATNESS OF THE POWER
WHICH IT EXHIBITS.

1. In saving from defilement of sin.
2. From the desire to sin.

3. From the dominion of sin.

IV. THE GREATNESS OF THE POSITION
TO WHICH IT EXALTS.

It makes us sons of God; heirs of glory.

V. THE GREATNESS OF THE PROSPECT
WHICH IT HOLDS OUT.

Assures us of heaven.

Appendix I

The Titanic's Last Hero: Reverend John Harper

As told by Lowell Lytle (portraying Captain Smith) at the Titanic Museum Attraction in Branson, Missouri and Pigeon Forge, Tennessee.

There were a lot of Heroes that night. Think of it! The Catholic priest giving the last rights till the very end. The band playing to the very end. The men standing back letting the woman and children board the lifeboats to the very end. HEROES ALL! But this one is special. Second Class passenger Reverend John Harper, a Scottish Baptist Minister on his way to Chicago to preach at Moody Memorial Church. He had preached there before and they wanted him back for three more months of meetings. It was a huge church and it is until this day. You must be good to preach there.

Reverend Harper thought he would take the *Lusitania* but changed his mind and decided to take the *Titanic*. While having an evangelistic program in Glasgow, Scotland one of his parishioners overheard him say he would take the *Titanic* and he prayed about it. He told Reverend Harper, "I have an ominous feeling about that ship. If you will take the *Lusitania* I'll pay for your ticket." Reverend Harper thought about it and said, "the apostle Paul wouldn't run away from danger, if anything happens I'm ready."

And it happened! When the *Titanic* started to go down Reverend Harper's faith was tested. This Baptist minister ran around the deck shouting "women and children and unsaved people get aboard the life boats." He even took off his life vest and gave it to a man that was not a believer in Jesus Christ. His sister-in-law and daughter, Nana, were standing next to him. They both survived. His sister-in-law over heard him when he gave the life vest to the man, he said "Take this . . . I don't need it . . . I'm not going down, I'm going *up*."

He's in the water now. No life vest. You would last for 10 to 40 minutes depending on your will to live and how much body weight you have. But all the cries and screams ended after 40 minutes. These people did not drown, THEY FROZE TO DEATH!

One man survived in a life boat. He lived in Detroit, Michigan and later on in years when he would go see the Detroit Tigers play and someone would hit a home run and the crowd would yell and scream, he said, "it was the same sound, I hated that sound."

Reverend Harper is now alone with no life vest. The water is 28 degrees. Salt water takes longer to freeze. It feels like a thousand knives stabbing you. A man drifted by on a piece of wood. Reverend Harper shouted to the man, "IS YOUR SOUL SAVED?" the man said, "NO." Reverend Harper shouted, "BELIEVE IN THE LORD JESUS CHRIST AND THOU SHALT BE SAVED." The man drifted off into the dark and later the current drew him back. Reverend Harper shouted again, "ARE YOU SAVED YET?" The man said, "I CAN'T

HONESTLY SAY THAT I AM." Reverend Harper shouted one more time, "BELIEVE ON THE LORD JESUS CHRIST AND THOU SHALT BE SAVED." And with that the Reverend slipped under the water and went to that frozen . . . watery . . . grave.

There were 12 people pulled from the water that night, six of them lived and that man was one of them. And the story was told a few weeks later in Hamilton, Ontario by that same man who said, "I LISTENED TO REVEREND HARPER'S LAST MESSAGE AND BECAME A BELIEVER IN JESUS CHRIST WITH TWO MILES OF WATER BENEATH ME."

Titanic's Last Hero, REVEREND JOHN HARPER.

Lowell Lytle

Appendix II

Moody Adams' "The Titanic's Last Hero" was originally published in 1997 and has been republished in several different formats over the years. Most of those printings seem to have been in the short-run or print-on-demand format similar to what you might find at some of the larger retailers. In any event, the book has not been readily available for the past several years.

The emphasis for this publication of Adams' stellar classic derived from listening to Lowell Lytle, who portrays Captain Smith, regale listeners with his *Titanic's Last Hero* story. Lowell presents the story several times a day when he is in residence at the Titanic Museum Attraction in Branson, Missouri, Pigeon Forge, Tennessee or one of the other numerous Titanic exhibits he frequents so often. Lowell has an uncanny resemblance to the real Captain Edward J. Smith and as I watch him and listen to him speak, I stand there in awe of this man who could be the real Captain Smith telling a story about John Harper, a relatively unknown man who was one of the true heroes of the *Titanic* tragedy.

So many men and women were heroes that night. We seem to remember the men who gave up their seats to others. Unless you have studied the *Titanic* story, you probably do not know about the women who also gave up their seats to others, or the numerous women who chose to remain behind with their husbands. Or the seven members of the clergy on *Titanic* when it sank. None of the seven survived. I think the John Harper story would probably be typical of all of them.

While long out of print, "The Titanic's Last Hero" is one of the most sought-after books in the gift shops at the *Titanic* exhibits. The original book was both inspiring and educational. My reprint has maintained the integrity of the book although it has been reformatted to remove 16 blank pages which earlier editions contained, allowing me to add in some editorial comments and historical information on the remaining pages. I was also able to include the full text of Lowell Lytle's famous *Titanic's Last Hero* speech in Appendix I.

Appendix II is my contribution to the Reverend John Harper and *Titanic* story while Appendix III are some of the human interest stories from *Titanic*. Most of the information has been extracted from my two books "1912 Facts About Titanic" and "Titanic Names: A Complete List of the Passengers and Crew." If you are interested in learning more about the *Titanic* disaster, you can obtain copies of either book at any of the Titanic gift shops, your favorite bookstore or, for a signed/autographed copy from me directly, email me at rocklinpress@earthlink.net.

Enjoy the book.

Lee W. Merideth
January, 2012

John Harper, daughter Nina and Jessie Leitch.

John Harper, Annie Harper and Jessie Leitch

John Harper was born in Scotland in 1872 and was 40 years old when he boarded *Titanic* as a Second Class passenger in Southampton, England. He was traveling to Chicago, Illinois to appear in a series of revival meetings at Chicago's Moody Church. Traveling with Harper was his six-year old daughter Annie Jessie Harper (known as Nan, Nana and Nina) and Miss Jessie Leitch, Nina's aunt.

Harper had been married to his wife Ann only two years when, on New Years Day 1906, little Annie was born. Within days Harper's wife died of complications of childbirth, so John Harper was left to raise Nina alone. To the rescue came Jessie Leitch, a 31-year-old unmarried woman to work as a nanny for the child. Consequently, when Harper decided to make the trip to Chicago, both Nina and Jessie accompanied him.

Harper managed to get both his daughter and Jessie loaded into Lifeboat 11 about one hour before *Titanic* sank. Lifeboat 11 was the first of just a few lifeboats that were loaded beyond capacity. Jessie was one of the survivors who had to stand several hours in the lifeboat until rescued by the *Carpathia*.

A week after arriving in New York City on the *Carpathia*, Nina and Jessie boarded a ship and returned to England. Nina was raised by Harper's brothers and was warned not to speak about the disaster. It wasn't until later years that she did so.

Eventually, Nina married a Baptist minister and remained in England until her death in 1986 at the age of 80. Nina was alive when the remains of the *Titanic* were discovered in 1985, but felt there was no reason to salvage any of the wreck.

Jessie Leitch eventually settled in Wales and married a gentleman from that country. He died in 1928. Jessie remained in Wales and died there in 1963.

The Harper Story Origins

In the scene near the end of the James Cameron movie *Titanic,* where a clergyman is hanging onto a piece of the ship and is giving absolution to those around him, is a composite of two clergymen loosely based on John Harper and Reverend Thomas R. D. Byles. However, Harper was seen or heard in the water by several survivors, most of whom were in the lifeboats.

George H. Cavell was a crew member who circulated the story about John Harper as being *Titanic's Last Hero.* Cavell was in Lifeboat 15 from the time it was launched, thus he was never in the water. It is quite possible he overheard Harper making the comment about "letting the women, children and unsaved into the lifeboat" since that recollection is attributed to Cavell. Several other survivors from Lifeboat 15 commented about some member of the clergy (in the panic, confusion and darkness, they didn't know who it was) giving absolution and offering prayers and forgiveness to those within hearing range for about 15 minutes until he either drowned or perished from the cold. That could have been Harper or someone else, although probably not Father Byles, who was known to be on the ship at the time it sank. If Cavell heard Reverend Harper from Lifeboat 15 which was launched 50 minutes before *Titanic* sank, that would eliminate Byles. We will never know for sure, but the story sounds like something an altruistic person like John Harper would have said and done.

Clergy on the *Titanic*

There were seven members of the clergy on *Titanic* when it sank, none of whom survived the sinking. They were:

Reverend Robert J. Bateman, 51, a Baptist Minister residing in Jacksonville, Florida. He traveled Second Class with this sister-in-law Mrs. Ada Balls. His body was recovered and he is buried in Jacksonville, Florida.

Father Thomas R. D. Byles, 42, a Catholic Priest residing in London. He was traveling Second Class to New York City to officiate in his brother's wedding.

Reverend Ernest C. Carter, 54, resided in London. He traveled with his wife Lilian to New York City. Neither survived the sinking.

Reverend John Harper, 39, a Baptist Minister residing in London. He traveled with his daughter Nina and his cousin Jessie Leitch. He was traveling to Chicago to begin a series of revival meetings.

Reverend William Lahtinen, 35, lived in Minneapolis, Minnesota and had been traveling to Finland with his wife Anna. Both were lost at sea.

Father Juozas (Joseph) Montvila, 27, from Lithuania, but lived in London and was emigrating to Worcester, Massachusetts.

Father Josef (Joseph) Peruschitz, 41, lived in Bavaria, Germany, and was traveling to St. Cloud, Minnesota to manage a Benedictine School.

Not included in the above list is probably one of the most famous members of the clergy who was on *Titanic* but got off in Queenstown. Thus Father Francis M. Browne was not on *Titanic* when it sank. As an amateur photographer, Browne is responsible for most of the photographs of *Titanic* in Southampton before she sailed, and all of the photographs taken of the passengers and crew during the voyage to Southampton. Many of them are on permanent display at various *Titanic* museums.

The 14 days of *Titanic*

Titanic put to sea under its own power on only two voyages: its sea trials from Belfast, Ireland and its departure from Southampton, England on its first passenger or maiden voyage. Both of those voyages, *Titanic's* entire career, lasted a total of only 14 days.

The two-week life of *Titanic* is as follows:

Tuesday, April 2, 1912: at 6:00 a.m. *Titanic* departed Belfast on its day-long sea trials. The ship and crew successfully pass the Board of Trade (BOT) trials and then *Titanic* steamed toward Southampton for its maiden voyage.

Wednesday, April 3: *Titanic* arrives in Southampton, England near midnight.

Thursday, April 4: throughout the day and evening, coal-bearing colliers tied up next to *Titanic* and finished loading the last of 6,300 tons of coal the ship would need to make the voyage to New York.

Friday, April 5 (Good Friday): once the coal dust had been wiped up, hundreds of workers installed much of the material that would be used by the passengers: china, furniture, linens, etc.

Saturday, April 6: most of the crew was hired. Hundreds of crew members were hired and were told to come back Wednesday morning.

Sunday, April 7 (Easter Sunday): all work was suspended so workers could spend time with their families.

Monday, April 8: most of the general cargo was loaded, as was much of the food and other consumables (beer, liquor, water, etc.)

Tuesday, April 9: all remaining cargo, food and consumables had to be loaded, all finish work (furniture, china, painting, etc.) was finished and hundreds of fresh plants and flowers were loaded.

Wednesday, April 10: departure day. The 700 crew hired on Saturday arrived by 6:00 a.m. to learn their assignments, find their work places and set to work. Each member of the crew would pass by a medical officer and then be "signed on." Two lifeboats were lowered and then raised back aboard. Around 9:30 the passengers started to board and the process would continue until 11:30. At noon everything was ready for departure and *Titanic's* huge whistles blew as the tugs pulled the ship away from the dock and its three enormous propellers began to rotate. *Titanic* headed for open water and its first port stop in Cherbourg, France, 67 miles and a few hours away.

Titanic put into Cherbourg around dusk and for the next few hours, 274 mostly First and Second class passengers were taken by boat out to *Titanic*, where they boarded. *Titanic* then departed Cherbourg en-route to Queenstown, Ireland.

Thursday, April 11: at 11:30 a.m. *Titanic* dropped anchor two miles off the coast of Queenstown, Ireland. Over 120 passengers boarded, eight departed and one crew member jumped ship. *Titanic* departed Queenstown at 1:45 p.m. and headed for the open sea, its next destination New York City.

Friday, April 12: the first full day at sea.

Saturday, April 13: the second full day at sea.

Sunday, April 14: Religious services were held throughout the ship. Several of the First Class passengers hosted a dinner for Captain Smith. Iceberg warnings had been received all day, as they had every day since leaving Southampton. Captain Smith decided to delay a major course change for a direct mid-ocean turn into New York by almost an hour to allow him to clear the known ice he was warned of by other ships. At 11:40 p.m., *Titanic* struck an iceberg.

Monday, April 15: at 2:20 a.m., two hours and forty minutes after striking an iceberg, *Titanic* sank two and a half miles to the bottom of the Atlantic Ocean. A total of 1,503 people died and another 705 were rescued by the *Carpathia*. Survivors were taken to New York City where they arrived late on the evening of April 18, 1912.

Titanic **Numbers**

There were 2,208 people on *Titanic* when it sank on April 15, 1912. Of those, 705 survived and the rest died in the freezing cold waters of the North Atlantic Ocean. Their numbers are as follows.

Class	Men		Women		Children		Total
	Saved	Lost	Saved	Lost	Saved	Lost	
First	59	118	136	4	6	1	324
Second	14	150	78	13	28	0	283
Third	59	387	83	87	31	63	710
Crew	193	677	19	2	0	0	891
Total	325	1332	315	106	65	64	2208